MORPHOSIS
BUILDINGS AND PROJECTS

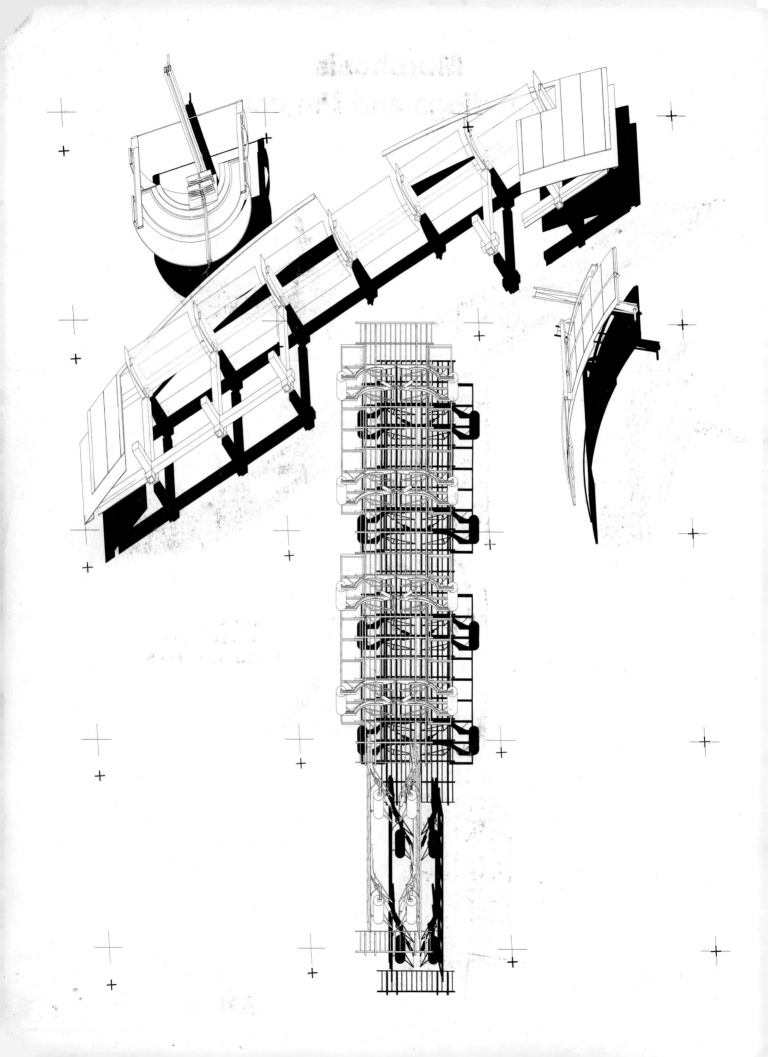

Morphosis
Buildings and Projects

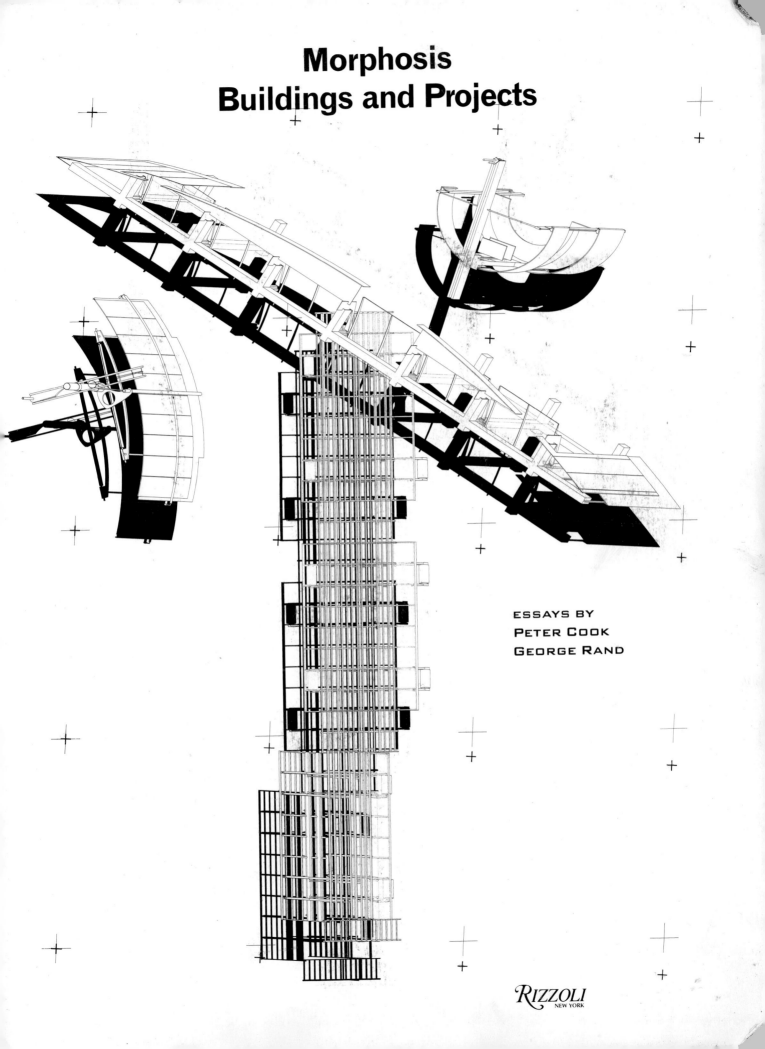

ESSAYS BY
PETER COOK
GEORGE RAND

RIZZOLI
NEW YORK

First published in the United States of America in 1989
RIZZOLI INTERNATIONAL PUBLICATIONS, INC.,
300 Park Avenue South, New York, NY 10010

Library of Congress Cataloging-in-Publication Data
Cook, Peter.
Morphosis: buildings and projects/Peter Cook, George Rand.
p. cm. Bibliography: p.
ISBN 0-8478-1030-5 – ISBN 0-8478-1031-3 (pbk.)
1. Morphosis Architects. 2. Architecture. Modern – 20th century-
California. I Rand, George. II. Title.
NA737.M72C55   1989   88-43453
720'.92'2 – dc20   CIP

DESIGNED BY LORRAINE WILD
Composition in Frutiger, Monotype Grotesque, and Bank Gothic by Continental Typographics,
Chatsworth, California
Printed and bound in Japan

Front cover: the orrery, Kate Mantillini Restaurant, 1987.

PHOTO CREDITS:

Aaron, Peter: p.86, top; p.90.

Assassi: pgs.154–157, all photos; pgs.208–209,
all photos.

Bishop, Roland; p.158.

Bonner, Tom: cover photo; p.61; p.64, all photos; p.75;
p.77; pgs.80–82, all photos; pgs.92–93, all photos;
pgs.104–105, all photos; p.110; pgs.112–113, all photos;
p.116, bottom right; pgs.117–121, all photos; p.130; p.131,
all photos; p.132–133, both photos, p.137, bottom photos;
p.138; p.139, bottom right; pgs.142–145, all photos; p.151,
center; pgs.152–153, all photos; pgs.166–167, all photos;
p.174–175, both photos; pgs.180–181, all photos; p.182,
bottom; p.183, center left and right; p.184, both photos;
p.187, top and bottom; p.188, top and bottom; p.189, top
eight photos; pgs.190–191, all photos; pgs.193–195, all
photos; pgs.198–203, all photos; p.205, top right; p.206,
both photos; p.210, center and bottom left; p.213, top left
and top right; pgs.214–215, all photos; p.216, all photos;
pgs.218–221, all photos; pgs.224–225, all photos; pgs.227–
229, all photos; pgs.232–233, both photos.

Blunck, Ranier: p.91 top and bottom; pgs.94–95, all photos;
pgs:102–103; p.108, top and bottom; p.111, top and center
right.

Daniels, Charles: p.150.

Hursley, Timothy: p.109; p.111, center left.

Irsonti, Gianluigi: p.68; p.70, top left; p.86, bottom left.

Mayne, Thom: p.8; p.16; p.54; p.234; p.236; p.239,
bottom.

McFarland, Brendon: p.128.

Morphosis: p.34; p.44; p.48; p.210, top left

Mudford, Grant: p.147, top; p.149.

Nichols, John: prints and photos, pgs. 230–231.

Rand, Marvin: p.40, bottom right; p.41; p.50, top right;
p.51; p.55; pgs.56–57; p.70, bottom right; p.71; p.73, all
photos; p.96, top and bottom, all photos.

R'Kul, Kanika: p.8; p.216, top right.

Street-Porter, Tim: p.40–41, all photos; p.126, top right;
p.134; p.135, top and bottom right; p.139, top left; p.140–
141; all photos.

Vertikoff, Alex: p.159, all photos; pgs. 160–161, all photos.

Warchol, Paul: pgs. 106–107, all photos; p.114; p.115, bottom left; p.116, top left; p.119, bottom right; p.122–p.125,
all photos; p.126, bottom left; p.127.

Zimbaldi, Daniel: pgs.30–31, all photos; p.39, all photos.

Foreword

In the late 1960s and early 1970s many schools of architecture were experimenting with ideas connected to notions of architecture as a quasi-scientific pursuit. There was a forward thrust propelling us into the future. Fundamental continuities were broken with regard to accepted notions of the basic requirements for the education of an architect (history and drawing, for example). The focus was on the holistic visions of a *rational approach* which paralleled a perception of scientific inquiry marked by an inherently circular integration of analysis and synthesis. As products of this system we lacked confidence, and were somewhat suspicious of the more intuitive potential of invention. Intellect and intuition had yet to be reintegrated into a single *modus operandi*.

Our early projects, notably the Sequoyah School and the Medical Office Building, were a direct response to this circumstance: the hunches were there, just not quite grasped. The focus was on infrastructures, with their emphasis on program, the environment, change and flexibility, and movement; the objective was a generic, neutral architecture resulting as a pure manifestation of these forces.

With the Venice houses we began a shift to more private and expressive concerns, focusing both on the making of visual and spatial connections between building and context and pursuing ideas which attempted to establish a dialogue between the idealized and the idiosyncratic characteristics inherent in each problem. The work was more and more about conflicts, questioning the normative and clashing with the expected; it was an intersecting of our subjective views and the programmatic demands of our clients. The grammatical rules were evolving. There was an intentional juxtaposition of unlike materials in conjunction with the use of a large number of parts and a purposeful interaction of structural and non-structural elements. Later projects such as the Crawford Residence and the 6th Street House continued to explore this dialogue through an increasingly complex or multi-layered strategy articulating the non-visual aspects of the work. There was an explicit connection to what was perceived as an indecipherable, pluralistic, and heterogeneous world. Emerging through the noise was an everpresent concern for *order*.

These projects, from our smallest scale commissions, such as the 2-4-6-8 House, attempt to comment on their urban situations; they are informed by the city and in turn aspire to redefine it. As extensions of their immediate site conditions, they participate in defining limits and boundaries and make both generalized and specific observations. Late projects, such as 72 Market Street and Kate Mantilini, pursue these interests within a more confrontational strategy. Buildings become interventions into an existing fabric as a means of experiencing the collision of the contemporary world while maintaining a consciousness of the past. Tradition and history are used as the groundwork for new organizational and conceptual ideas in a time when much of architecture is preoccupied with accomplishments from the past and their *literal* interpretations.

We reiterate the dialogue between the general and the specific at the site as the work responds to accommodation. We're developing a direct discourse about the connection (or disconnection) between use and form, which questions both the priority of function within the design process and the assumption that the satisfaction of our needs is the most important goal. Technology supports use, not the other way around. The issue is to develop a definition of appropriateness while questioning current notions regarding the optimization of technology. The tectonic focus of our work is about making (sometimes unmaking) and communicating the process and activity of construction. It utilizes the inherent qualities of materials and the expression of that materiality to produce a building's particular quality (it's "authenticness"). There is a deliberate tension created between the simplicity and the generic nature of materials and the abstract/conceptual nature of the work as a whole. We reject the current convention that equates value with the preciousness of materials over the transcendence of the concept. Ideas of luxury, or value, are represented by the richness of form as it manifests concepts. Beauty is thus a consequence of a profound intimacy with material things; it cannot be possessed beyond the moment; it is reclusive, inexplicable, and unreproducible.

Architecture is, finally, a means of communication, a way to describe things for which words are inappropriate or inaccurate, and to speak about the culture from which it comes. We take a point of view. Our work concretizes the ephemerality of feeling. It transcribes the complexities of the world and the fragmented, disbursed, and detached nature of existence. Our interest in indeterminacy parallels our interest in formal language. Our work reiterates the unfinished nature of things. We hope it unmasks the deceptions of first appearance and explores what we don't see.

Thom Mayne/Michael Rotondi
Santa Monica, October, 1989

7

8

1998. # The Chemistry of Architecture

The chemistry of architecture is a beautiful fascination, but do we really understand it? Are we not too eager to ascribe those strange juxtapositions of bits and pieces of the familiar—roofs, gables, garden walls and things for people to peek out of or slip discreetly into—to the reasonable business of being accommodated, sheltered, built-for? It seems though, that we miss a lot of the magic of the creative process when we merely overlay the *stated* additional games played by the designer or overlay some of our favorite classroom prejudices. So it is that observances of Historic Icons, Philosophical Allusions, Geometric Tricks are there for the picking, but still miss the positive quality of *coincidence* which is somehow related to the inherent quality of *collage*.

That the Morphosis pair of Thom Mayne and Michael Rotondi are aware of this mysterious extra territory is given away in a snippet from Mayne's own description of their objectives in the 6th Street House—as searching for the *"ability to absorb the idiosyncratic."* You don't have to be much of a cynic, more an open-eyed observer of life to realize that most urban existence in the late twentieth century is the absorption of the idiosyncratic; and just as we expect an engaging novelist or journalist to be able to extract the telling or the quizzical out of the apparent normality of life, and in the same way expect an illustrator or film-maker to lean the eye towards such things, then why not an architect?

We can ponder the fascination that Wittgenstein's one excursion into architecture has for us: not enough to note objectively that a none-too-exceptional modernist structure with some quite straightforward characteristics must be chewed-over from window to window, corner to corner, so as to absorb the (presumed) thoughts and significances and then conclude that, after all, architecture was not *his* language. I believe that the composition of a piece of architecture can develop quite strong narrative lines and layers within *its* language: with the work of Morphosis there are continual clues in their obvious knowledge of, and sometimes fascination with, their clients, which can also be the inspiration. The language is of a special degree of abstraction: unlike the writer, it need not restrict its documentation to that lineality and musical sense of the "digestible" read. Unlike the painter, it is not necessary to summon-up all the forces in a single, memorable image. Succinctness is not necessarily a quality of all good architecture. Only of some.

But the narrative layer is only one. There is the functional.

How marvellous it is to be, at last, far enough away from the period of history where the acknowledgement of function need not involve us in honoring it. An approach to the business of getting people in and out of a building, giving them enough space to do what they must do and then, perhaps as a bit of an indulgence, celebrating some particular commonplace activity—maybe it's collecting books, or keeping cats or having a view of the sea or doing aerobics—with a special altarpiece. From this moment on, the air begins to fill with these collaged absorptions of the idiosyncratic, and dare one say it: the idiosyncrasies are deliberately created as well as absorbed.

That special architecture *should* come out of Los Angeles has been one of the excuses for my twenty-year love affair with the city. That this particular repository of the invented world, the dreamed-up world and the instantly summonable environment, should—and must—have its effect upon the local architects is obvious. But my first joyous reactions at seeing the audacities of John Lautner or the cuteness of Lloyd Wright have been progressively overlaid by watching the younger, the *real* Angeles architects. I suspect that to them, the snide dismissals of earlier years and the bright-eyed chasing after toy architecture that is the indulgence of grey Easterners and phased Europeans is an equal avoidance of the issue. A city of such rich cultural mix and girth and such curious overlay of the commonplace issue of drilling for oil or making airplanes or selling software, with quaint lurches into forgotten attempts at escape (usually from the Midwest) that have left baked-up pensioners tapping around their yard as lonely and puzzled as they might be in old Zagreb—what should it really have to offer as its alternative to the Georgian terrace or to the Grands Boulevards or to the bourgeois villa?

Increasingly there seems to be a parallel wish for seriousness and reason as *a priori* to the relaxed absorption of beachtown gambitry. Moreover, this gambitry is, on closer inspection, more an attitude towards hardware than merely the reproduction of forms and techniques borrowed from beach and strip. The portfolio of Los Angeles junk architecture concerns itself with legitimate breakdowns between roof and wall, vegetation and enclosure, tack-on and dig-in, and a most extraordinary attitude

9

towards the ground plane as befits slide areas and swamps and inhospitable cliffs. From this one can then affect a delicious overlay of any mixture being possible, the creative effect of cutting (in film) with its speed and callousness which, if extrapolated, could have dramatic consequences to the otherwise gentlemanly way in which most architecture concerns itself with cause-and-effect—the "after you Charles" consistencies that can even be felt in Russian Constructivism, if you are familiar with the language of its parts.

The clue is in one of the earliest built works of Morphosis, the "2-4-6-8 House," a building that sets up a conversation with itself. It is a camera offering a series of peeks out to the flotsam and jetsam of backyard Venice, at once part of it and aloof from it, for the bright paintwork and the sign-like quality of the separated wooden parts makes light of its self-awareness. A schoolmarm finding herself in an ice cream line smiles brightly at first glance, but then she is to be seen peering quizzically through the deliberate frames of (in this case) four sets of spectacles.

Could this selfconsciousness also be a selfpossessedness that must come from two young architects who were spending a great deal of their time as teachers, rationalizing and postrationalizing the issues of architecture *as such* for other young architects? Few clues can be found from the earlier built work in Tijuana, at least not expressionistically; for there the strong, stark walls and reduced fenestration act only to establish sharply the diagram of the building and its concentration upon the walled rectangle of space that allows itself to be invaded by a house for roughly 50 percent of its space. The only ponderable is the architects' statement that it is a "straightforward, systematic approach to row housing…required by Chermayeff and Alexander's classic book *Community and Privacy*. In fact, the Morphosis work never looked as direct and scholarly and (though in Mexico) *European* again. One is fascinated, as one was in seeing Arata Isozaki's early girls' school in his home town of Oita, or Gunther Domenig's teachers' training college in Graz (before the explosions of the "Z" bank and so-on). These buildings are, all of them, textbook examples of direct planning, and good spaces, and, more significantly, the placing of walls are only where they need to be. It is perhaps our preoccupation with facade (helped along by a generation of critics

keen to find pictorial-verbal icons rather than delve around the more labyrinthine conditions of a building), that concentrates our attention on windows and doors, surfaces and viewable assemblages. These early buildings by highly inventive architects do, in fact, contain the wit of invention and ability to wring out of normal events the stuff of architecture. In all three cases, it will become more and more useful to return and ignore (perhaps) their own irritations with this *direct* and unfashionable work.

Was it in Mexico that the young teachers were able to build directly on a tight budget in a culturally ambiguous territory? Did they manage to work out those same exercises that young English or Dutch architects worked out vis-a-vis le Corbusier via Atelier 5? The section of the Tijuana houses reveals an understanding of light—full light, peered-at light, borrowed light. Without having been there, one senses the quality of coolness, very much allied to this sense of calm and the shielding wall.

What makes the "2-4-6-8" admirable is its concentration upon one key idea and lack of nervousness about this concentration. In the twelve years since, the world of architectural discussion has virtually exploded and a more histrionic mood has taken over, not least inspired by Morphosis' "uncle," Frank Gehry. It would be out of character for Mayne or Rotondi to wear their psychological or artistic hearts on their sleeves in the way that Frank can. Yet in his case, the cut and thrust of commercial survival was interwoven amongst a conscious involvement in the artistic milieu of Los Angeles and was at a level of contrast, even rhetoric, that doesn't now seem necessary to the generation in their late thirties or mid forties. The role of the "new" and loose-limbed school, SCI-ARC (Southern California Institute of Architecture), where Mayne was one of the original teachers and Rotondi was one of the first graduates and is present director, has served their work instead. Having observed them in class as well as in the office, I am struck by the way in which the quizzical attitude towards architectural inheritance can be carried forth from the one to the other. Simple rhetoric or "naughty boy" roles are thus seen as being too simplistic and able to be replaced by layers and layers of criticism and a clarification of discussion so that the point of departure of one of their buildings can be intensively stated. Much of their energy in the years of the last decade has gone into helping to create, out of a laid-back and sweetly renegade institution, a place where some of the most investigative younger architects are gravitating in order to be intelligently criticized, so their own acridity as critics develops: it has to be self-imposed as well as pedagogically effective. It can lead to selfconsciousness, of course, so that one of their least memorable projects, the Western-Melrose Offices, can remain in the mind as a verbally stated idea for: "the typological nature of walls in order to address both conceptual and practical issues. First, the wall produces a prominent corner for a building on a prominent site. Second, the wall type changes to scale the building to its context. Third, the changing wall refers to the merging of two different types while deferring to existing buildings. Finally, this layered surface is used for sun control by the addition of retractable blinds." Basically, at this time (1980), they are waiting for the chance really to overlay a series of scalar or recognitive ideas into something larger than a yard house. That Kate Mantilini's Restaurant or the Cedars Sinai Medical Center can, by their complexity and mandate, rise to the audacity of the brave words of the Western-Melrose, and more, sets up a nagging question.

Too often we can separate the pomposity of academics discussing architecture from the territory of the quick job for the money man. More complexedly, we can separate the aspirations of the eager, angry, territorially frustrated young architect from the punch-taking steps of the operational, but still aggressive and good, architect. Very good architects do somehow hold on to it all. Why can't a corner wall for a developer be an essay in expressionism? Why can't the demand for rationale made in a seminar be the same demand for rationale directed towards the devoted assistant at twelve o'clock at night? The strength of the Morphosis work of the last eight years is that it has intelligently *rolled* with the academic/intellectual punches of the SCI-ARC experience and allowed the pragmatics of construction and cost limitation to be supporting conditions. As the tide of architectural discussion has turned away from the quasi-historic or the purely rational towards the spatial and the explosive, Morphosis has expanded its system of creative nets into which it can hold several coincident conversations. Of course, the tricky patch was during the time that this sophistication of understanding was building up, yet the jobs themselves remained small.

First smatterings of such a dilemma rest even in the Sedlak House addition. Just down the track from the "2-4-6-8," it purports "coherent ideal, to emerge conceptually from the contingent topiary." It is delightful enough as an object, but nobody is fooled by the words; it is almost surely a very small and restricted shell desperately wishing to be spatially as well as nominally as contrapuntal as the description suggests. The carcass (I think for the first time in their work) shifts significantly, but the shift is as much an itch as it is a quote. In a sense, the Flores house expansion finds a more appropriate texture for its conceptual language. The project here is also modest—a mere lateral expansion—and held, more-or-less achieved, in a series of parallel layers of wall. All that intervenes is a drift of stair and toilet intervention: that is all that is needed. An almost copybook exercise, it prefaces the time when the walls can act both as a conversation with each other as layers and as the scenic contrivance for gatherings of idiosyncratic individuals, the clientele of Kate Mantilini's Restaurant.

In level of sophistication, intensity of programmatic and editorial sense, and academic exercising on a larger scale than previously available, the Lawrence House at Hermosa Beach is the key turning point. It is seized upon by Morphosis as a chance really to set up two component forces that can act upon each other with enough space and enough objectives of recognition to start a real dialogue. There is the object that they describe as the "House" (an asphalt-shingled, gable-roofed structure set symmetrically in the site in memory of a house that once stood in its place), and the "Block"...a rectilinear box that slices through the diagonal, referring to some of the buildings around. When one looks at the plans and walks around the building itself, however, one realizes that this program is but a trigger for the very complex overlay of ideas. There is clearly a heroic spatial focus in the form of the half-circle shaft halfway along the north side, and it attracts much of the staircase activity. It has neoclassical aspirations, but only up to a point, for it opens off an alley and it has only wayward relationships to the principal rooms (which are anyway on a different axis). The mixture of rhetoric and calm, heroics and nonchalance, are to be found all over the building. A most revealing diagram is the *unfolded elevation* which clearly illustrates a most mature ability to control window series without becoming pious. The house is firm and centralized but has introspective fenestration, whereas the block is extrospective and its fenestration—makes a total diagrammatic statement. This must be read as a serial composition in which the total rectangle is directly related to the window opening—in analysis very similar to the game played by Richard Meier in his controlled requotation of Asplund's Villa Snellman at his Frankfurt Museum.

The framing of views, the threading of routes through and beyond the ceremonial shaft, and a straightforward attitude towards the big, useable volumes as well, make this one of the most urbane villas of recent times. In Hermosa Beach of all places!

It is at this point that Mayne and Rotondi's sense of theater as well as their obvious enjoyment of more cerebral architectural conversations becomes apparent. They will talk about the Lawrences, who are obviously a sophisticated enough couple to provide plenty of constituent material for the layered idiosyncrasies of family commonplaces and conscious activities to be overlaid. The house can be worn as a party piece or it can inhabited as an elegant beach house. I guess, should the need arise, that it could be used as a series of temporary retreats or assertions of different moods or postures that always do occur in family life. It is rare for a modern building of its size to have the quality of comprehendibility along with so many nooks and crannies. Its greyness does not appeal to me, though it probably has its own buzz for Angeles folk; to a European who sees enough grey it feels that it could just as happily been white and, as an excuse, the cartographic discussion of its facades could have been even more clearly spelled out. The galvanized steel and the tack-on felt tiles have the last say for other reasons, of course; they are the children of the time, of the budget, and of the deliberate wish to avoid the danger of prissiness which would never occur to one in a European museum park but might be terribly wrong in a California beach town. Here then is an essay in raunch as well nonchalance. The academics have come out of hiding and are becoming as streetwise as Uncle (Frank Gehry).

Concurrent with this work were the many projects that became known through publications, though never built, so there began to be a recognition of the Morphosis ethos through their marvellous models and drawings. The models in particular have a distinctive characteristic of being bas-reliefs in the antique mode. I refuse to believe that this well worked-over patina of paint is not a strange instinctive grab at a quality that one has experienced once or twice inside a Roman villa or in sniffing at the original drawings for the thesis works in the 19th century Ecole des Beaux-Arts—some feeling of status mixed with solidity; some quality of the *established*—in tactile form. One can ponder this instinctive need if you come from Los Angeles and wish to be part of the creation of a serious architecture for that town, of a good architecture—to be *in* the hillside, to be *of* it, rather than sliding off the side and rolling away, to be *hewn* instead of always being tacked together. Perhaps it is in reverse, the same instinct that inspired so many twentieth century architects of imagination in Northern Europe to crave for glass, for the glimpse of the sun, to eschew the tyranny of the dank wall and the solid column. So it is quite legitimate to analyze drawings, models, and the deliberate stylization of their elegant distortions in order to pry open just *what* the taste and aspirations of the designers might be. The models can be read as art pieces in their own right. They can be read as distillations of the analytical technique of layering (and some of the models are very deliberately set up in this way). They can be read as invitations to note the primary intentions of the building before being sidetracked by the context or the built materials. Out of it all has come a very astute ability with walls. No longer mere dividers of space or lines of force, they increasingly become musical combs where the interval between piers can be infinitely and subtly tuned. Another analogy might be that of a rack or of a loom where the existence of the spatial and "musical" interval is awaiting the insertion (or even counterpoint) of additional elements. Clearly, in some cases, these elements can be people themselves. By the time of the design of the Crawford house (the late 1980s) this accumulated method of modelling, combing, space-interval implosion, or whatever, has led to a peculiarly personal architectural mode. Moreover, it is one that can be put out in space and turned as the Crawford project enjoys showing.

The business of discussing architecture, explaining architecture, refining the discussion, refining the model, explaining the model, and *then* but only then, stretching and twisting the methodology seems to be the accumulative process by which the later Morphosis work is so assured and effectively grounded.

It is the very opposite of "knee-jerk" architecture.

In an unguarded moment, Michael Rotondi admitted that "young people have a sense of frustration and powerlessness, and there are times that I don't feel that different . . . because we too are looking for how to express ourselves, our work has a quality of questioning, of risk-taking. . . ." Admittedly, this was said a-propos the Market Street Restaurant and thus seems to summarize a frenetic period in their development. The necessary requirement of a restaurant to show-off could also be a nagging irony in the minds of such architects. At Market Street, it is necessary to set up a totally artificial range of atmospheres, analogous to the artificiality of the traditional theater stage, and somewhat in that tradition they established a "hot room" and a "cool" room. In the first, the geometry and iconography arrest and disorientate; in the second, they reassure once more. Reference and incident in one, near blandness in the other. Studio discussions can be exercised in such a restaurant. The restauranteur, by the way, can, if he wishes, bask in the knowledge that some of the great *experiential* leaps of the twentieth century have been made in restaurants. Imagine the bumptious diners of Berlin as they had to avoid glancing up at Wœurzbach and Belling's extraordinary ceiling (it's one thing to buy a neat little Finsterlin drawing, another thing to eat under it). By 1926 the rhetoric was out in the open, and even the cultural ambiguity of a Strasbourger must have been sorely stretched by van Doesburg's Aubette. Yet most unlikely of all is to imagine the stiff bourgeoisie of Stockholm finding themselves in a gossamer-loose cage such as Asplund's Paradise restaurant at the 1930 Exposition. These examples all went far beyond the accepted band of tolerance of their city and society at the time.

Yet, here we are in Los Angeles. All is tolerated. All those dreams have been put on celluloid. The Brown Derby is a thirty year old conversation if not more. The house developed in the yard of a tolerant intellectual is one thing, but the marketing of a space that you can chat about to your friends is another. I dwell upon the contradictory instinct that must have pressed in on Morphosis to some purpose: The need to show off; the wish to avoid beachtown gimmickry; the doubt perhaps that their accumulated vocabulary could be too obscure, even too tasteful; the reasoned instinct that knows that it must be possible to transfer qualities of scale, progression, hierarchy, and *then* dramatic incident somehow into a very public place where contemplation as such is not the mode.

Kate Mantilini's is the convincing response.

The strategy is of treating the existing building shell as a cage and then layering a new box within the cage—but much more. An almost ecclesiastical device emerges in their major work. The heroic shaft of the Lawrence house was an anticipation. The pillar game at Market Street another anticipation. But it requires a gesture as essentially theatrical and audacious as the introduction of the orrery object to set it all off. What we have here is a chapel or church dedicated to meeting and eating. The space is large enough to allow the swung geometry to hang there *in its place:* at the necessary position in the hierarchy of the architecture. Hung, swung, and essentially *commenting* upon the primary conditions rather than fragmenting them. The play of light is beautiful, the large mural is essential, the mystery of the orrery disappearing up into the sky is referred to by the authors as an "interpretive" project.

It seems though, that with all the accumulated wit of play, this building is powerful because it consciously or subconsciously understands the power of objects to set up just the right amount of play between themselves. In order for this to work they have to be elegantly balanced and then *telling*, and not just elegant. The pressed-out and wrapped bas-relief wall, the spider-like altarpiece, the tweak and tantalization of the occasional voluptuous surface, the usefulness of the absolutely regular and ordinary table layout as a regulator—put this all together and one is reminded of the balanced apparatus of the basilican church affected by Gothic tricks. Light, curvaceous occasions, layers of pierced wall—it's all there.

13

A serious restaurant might seem a curious artifact on the main street of Beverly Hills, but it is a question of timing as well. Just at the point where Morphosis might have been getting most frustrated with the tribulations and limitations of designing restaurants (a whole trail of them and all of them successful), this project emerges to vindicate the whole effort. Did they consciously attack it in a different way, or was it just a question of scale? Anyway, it remains in one's mind as having that enduringly European atmosphere of Oslo's Theatercafeen or the old Coupole in Montparnasse—a response to the essentially theatrical nature of meeting and eating downtown.

Though two years separate the completion of Kate's and the Cancer Center for the Cedars-Sinai hospital, it seems essential to discuss them together. The mood with which one enters each could not, of course, be more different. The one with relaxed anticipation, the other with nervous apprehension. The one tripping casually off the street, the other disappearing down into a hole in the ground. Yet, in each, one is immediately struck by the role of the major space and the iconic object. Whether intended purely as a decoy or a focus, the play structure has a clear architectonic role in the Cancer center as did the orrery in Kate's. The comparison continues: the side walls of the restaurant are an essay in fragility and ambiguity; in the Center they are an excavation into the earth, moreover, an earth that we know contains some private and probably scary goings-on. Yet there is a certain matter-of-factness about the latter building that is engaging—the use of decoration at the focal points of corridors, the use of plate glass to prevent excessive secrecy and mystery where it would oppress even further. The clever utilization of such natural light as is available, so that you don't in the end feel that claustrophobic. There are 45 feet of height for the layering of the main space walls and the great deluge of light to be appreciated. From the plans we can trace another sophistication, whereby the swung geometries are acting as introductory conditions, "mouths," but then the inner conditions settle down to necessary foursquare hierarchies. In this building, too, the role of attached or dangled elements, such as lamps, arrive at a degree of finesse combined with *repetition* that inevitably recalls Otto Wagner's Post Office Savings Bank in Vienna. A clue, perhaps, to the issue of imaginatively speculative cities: only now can Los Angeles in general, and architects such as Morphosis in particular, have thrown out enough

strands of theatrical or literate design for them to be shaken down, structured to a degree, and set up as a new set of references.

In other words, the relative calmness and maturity of this piece reassures one that it can offer a total vocabulary of response.

In the light of that, the most recent houses and smaller projects become quite relaxed. But never boring.

Thom Mayne describes the design of the 6th Street project (a house) as continuing their "investigation of the impacted building; a metaphor for veils and walls that we use to protect ourselves from the world and the secrets and mysteries that are so much part of the human condition." Mayne's written descriptions of the work are often very poetic in themselves, and the available drawings push out into a twitching, restless condition where odd pieces of machine and roof and frame and stair are all exploding off the carcass. So not only is the impacted cage evolving, but is (at least theoretically) engaged in a wrestling match with specially invited parts. The orrery and the play structure from the larger works have their progeny here, but seem to be multiplying. Along with the assured quality of the overall carcass there is the restlessness of these small parts. At this moment, one starts to question the role of the model. If the eventual building feels like that object, it will have the compositional resolution of, say, Frank Lloyd Wright's better houses or of a De Stijl piece. But if the container can be persuaded to accept and ignite a series of restless metal parts, what then? Is there a robot or a ghost or a strange fluttering bat awaiting the next generation of Morphosis houses?

This activity level spreads to the whole concept where the Crawford house for Montecito is concerned, though here it seems to concern their favorite, and most developed, territory: the combs have now become staves as well as sheets of sound (in musical terms). An analysis of a piece of rich scoring might throw up something similar, where the interval of one coloration is hung in front of the interval of another and the melody line swung through. They offer their own program: "Arithmetic progression of pylons (totems), structure and walls determine the basic elements of the architecture. The same progression, but in reverse order, determines the size and character of the negative spaces between the elements."

A first glance at some of the drawn diagrams suggests a sideways observation of the explosive effect of Daniel Libeskind and his followers; and an academic conclusion might be that the Libeskind effect upon many of us is to encourage us to engage more relaxedly in the scattering as well as the layering of idiosyncratic series than we might have done before. Yet unlike Libeskind, the Morphosis partnership is quite able to *anchor* and at the same time *explode*. The key is a glance at the straightforward upper and lower level plans of this house. The existence of the arc wall as a kind of lasso is very engaging; the skimming quality of many of the marks made by the parts is captured in the dismembered model. Once again, we know that they are up to something *additional* to the known vocabulary—this time to do with lightness.

We can by now itemize some typical conditions of this architecture: the comb, the implosion, the church, the icon, the dangle, the shift across space between combs, the dig-in.

In a conclusive homing-in, I prefer to look back three or more years to a house, Venice III, which one simply enjoys for itself. It wears its heart well outside its sleeve: the restless wires and counterweights and sails are nonetheless resolved back onto the vertebrae of the house. The swung double-carcass that by now one has come to expect in Morphosis's work is pitched just at the right scale and right amount of incident. The bookshelves really are a celebration of the activity of the inhabitant, but remain also as an absorbent element; even the whiff of neoclassicism is relaxedly worn: as the imprint of the two-tented pyramids falls down to the ground it is picked up on a screen at one end and a dais at the other.

It is a building which is prepared to quote several of the parts of other Morphosis work: the galvanized faces from Lawrence, much of the "feel" of Mantilini (even though such a small house), even recollections of the earlier Venice backyard houses; but there is something additionally elegant about it. I am amused, by the way, that magazines very rarely show the adjoining bungalow, for the juxtaposition of the two (used as one building anyway) is not that bad. The real architectural statement is the *stronger* because they exist together. The ramshackle quality of Venice-as-found is lovingly and simultaneously regarded *and* disregarded. The schoolmarm has taken off her glasses and begun (almost coquettishly) to play with her companions. A shrill laugh and a few muttered literary quotations are uttered (of such a level of cultural elevation that they could not possibly be understood by the crowd) but said without bitchiness. Then, finally, the girlish revelation of bare shoulders. Something about this house suggests that from now on, Morphosis is happy with its literature: very precise with its scaling, and able to resist the overloading of certain nooks and crannies with too many decoys; naughty enough to put the most volatile elements on the *outside* of the building, and relate them (if they wish) to the most straightforward part of the plan.

We are back, are we not, to the layering of the idiosyncratic?

It would seem that in this instance, there was the ideal client. Not just a sponge for witty gambits but a true fan. Bright enough to ask creative questions. This was probably much in mind when the design was made.

In the next phase, a whole scale of activity remains to be explored. The urban scale projects for Hermosa Beach and other California locations are more diagramatically simple than one might expect. Yet Crawford is surely a model for an urban-scale intervention? Most recently, the Berlin architectural milieu was surprised (and not a little humbled) by the directness, and at the same time the poise of the "wall" project—a comment upon social interaction, a comment upon expressionistic directness, the most mature architecture to come out of Los Angeles since the Eames House, in a way with the same gravity, reminiscent of the 1960's as a proposition and as a form, yet utterly fresh in its manipulation and clarity.

There is now a sonority as well as a wit abroad in Santa Monica. The sonority has come as a result of their constant *consideration* of architecture, coming, as I have suggested, as much from their ability as critics as from the day-to-day office discussions. The wit has come from a quartet of extremely amused eyes blinking lovingly at the idiosyncracies of such a quaint city.

15

Morphosis: "formation" "in formation" "information"

One of the key challenges post-modern architecture has set for itself is the historical integration of past and present. To achieve this union, post-modern tapestries are woven of elements with contradictory associations. The post-modern "double coding" permits the blending of current and traditional fragments, pieces of diverse cultures, into new images which retain the scent of a common past. Part of the yearning of the post-modern mind, expressed in all the arts and particularly in literature, is the desire to openly reveal the weaving process itself. This includes seeing tattered edges, that is, showing the work for what it is, a deliberately constructed reality, a textual intervention shorn of the naturalizing tendencies of traditional narratives.

There is more to this impulse than merely revealing the process in the making. It implicitly recognizes the limits of individual personhood, our ability to create meaning apart from the social world. The post-modern personality is comprised of a series of "alterities," (a concept introduced by Soviet literary critic Mikhail Bakhtin)—multiple situated identities which long for a single center. The diverse cultural milieu can no longer hope for an underlying grammar to account for its manifold appearances. Changes from era to era, once taken to be an ever accumulating past, no longer mark us as inheritors of the roots of Western thought. The narrative text is completed and shaped into a coherent performance only by social exchange: in the case of personality development by interactions between self and other; in the case of history by the mutual interpretations of one culture by another.

Applying this thesis, the language of architecture will never achieve the identity for which it longs, an enduring reflection of that ancient Greek *Gemeinschaft* from which all subsequent history has been a falling away. In the "dialogic view" we are each only authors of events which require the response of other cultures to define their wholeness.

Once inherited styles are separated from their religious and cultural origins, we run the risk of the Nietschean alternative, a "ruthless forgetting" which ignores the past altogether and treats meaning as a function of arbitrary associations. Some post-modernists employ the past to project a "civic faith" (as in the official culture), that ultimately we will be able to resolve the multiple contradictions of wealth and poverty, race and gender. Charles

Moore's Beverly Hills Civic Center is emblematic of this belief that harmony can be achieved by inventing visual "neologisms"—for example, housing the bureaucracy in buildings clothed in images of a bygone civic culture, combining bits of the Quaker meeting house, a touch of the Alhambra, and strains of a far-off Italian piazza. The artistically unified and visually appealing product suggests that underlying political and economic divisions need no longer exist.

Morphosis assumes a harder line, going as far as a psycho-analytic style of self-confrontation. Rather than ironically bemoaning the loss of the canonic purity of the column as a universal figure of representation, they expand the "dialogic circle" to include popular culture.

The digital environment increasingly resembles a flickering text of pre-edited parts, subject to instant obliteration or recoding with the press of a button. Even national boundaries are subject to blurring due to the easy movement of money and resources by international capital (Lasswell, The Signature of Power). Ethnic distinctions are diffused by virtue of being mutually embedded in a sea of television and advertising (Merelman, *Making Something of Ourselves*; Lears, *"The Concept of Cultural Hegemony"*), no longer connected to their regions of origin.

"…all fixed, fast-frozen relations…are swept away."
COMMUNIST MANIFESTO

"Men's minds seek a simple truth, an answer which delivers them from their questions, a gospel, a tomb. The moments of refinement conceal a death principle: nothing is more fragile than subtlety."
SUSAN SONTAG, As quoted in Jerry Kosinski's *The Hermit of 69th Street: The Working Papers of Norbert Kosky.*

The point of departure for the designs of Morphosis is to be found in the intense individual concentration and self-evident solutions of Le Corbusier. Le Corbusier abstracted to the essence the radical effects of telephone communication, aerial images of the landscape, and mass transit, all of which dissolved the order of space and time that was considered to be "natural" at that time. Morphosis extends the Corbusian orthodoxy by employing a new set of "figures" or "tropes" related to contemporary media such as "stop action" and "instant replay" conventions of sports television, or the weaving together of fact and fiction in modern "docu-dramas." Their affection for found urban artifacts disrupts the presumed coherence of the ideology, the texts and images of the contemporary urban milieu.

17

Unlike early moderns, however, the environment faced by current artists can not assume the background of an agreed upon set of linguistic conventions. The sense of surprise and outrage 'fin de siecle' artists were able to evoke came from violating the expectations of an aesthetically comfortable, socially insulated Viennese culture. Schoenberg's tonal experiments took as implicit the perceived universality of the chromatic scale and confronted listeners with musical objects generated by means of a new and arbitrary grammar.

Playful reversals and inversions in current architecture can not assume a single classical tradition. More likely, the basis for generating "accidentals" (the equivalent of unpredictable "Wagnerian" contrasts) is in relation to formal elements used in popular media, image montages on MTV, erratic clothing combinations which reverse over-and under-garments, culinary tastes that mix and match distant traditions, new dance-steps and hallucinogenic states of mind. These formal elements are directly tied to emotions: quick and sharp rhythmic breaks, unexpected modulations, hesitancies and redundancies, incessant repetition. They are close to the anthropological language of the street, gestures of everyday human action, the by-products of many cultural forces brought into close proximity. Each culture responds to the metaphorical meanings and surface features of others to generate a polyglot aesthetic domain. Unlike canonic classicism with its striving for perfection, the designs of Morphosis evince a certain amount of intentional awkwardness. Like Borromini resisting the Pope, there is an effort to shy away from easy confidence and relaxed familiarity exuded by members of the dominant culture: no simple divisions into major and minor axes, or hierarchies. In short, the stridency of contemporary "rock and roll" does not produce "singable tunes"; Morphosis does not produce "sketchable designs."

"Comfort in their surroundings" evinced by American mainstream society has been achieved by spatial buffering of the self from the surrounding milieu, the separation of the well to do from the less well off. In other parts of the world, such as Latin America, it is common to see military guards positioned to protect homes of the wealthy from adjacent barrio dwellers.

The Los Angeles of the eighties is less spatially buffered than before, bringing unfamiliar patterns of speech and life styles into closer contact. In a polyglot aesthetic culture, there are no easily agreed upon traditions! Rap music is "demanding." Heavy metal strains for "energy release." Asian aesthetic styles value emotional containment and assertion of humility. The common ground is aesthetically enriched by the variety of responses produced in relation to the single act.

The personality of Morphosis designs reflects this backdrop. Parts are all in place, but the resultant ensemble has a slightly detached character, like the awkward stance of a body dancing backwards struggling to maintain equilibrium while preventing itself from falling. The work is characterized by contrasting modes of emotional expression: bold yet self-effacing, focusing on expressing the feeling of adequacy, yet humble. Energy is expressed and yet contained within the boundaries of classical rectangles rather than piercing the wall (as in Coop Himmelblau).

While their work can project an air of mystery, the user is made to feel complicit. Dense layers of accessible details invite the user to mentally participate in the logic of construction of the environment, an allegory about the way it is put together, rather than being seduced by it into unconscious appreciation.

"rulers do not dance" (because this is an act of being caught up in a mass movement, surrendering one's self to the environment...) IRWIN STRAUSS, *Phenomenological Psychology.*

"The inferno of the living is not something that will be:...There are two ways to escape suffering it. The first is easy for many: accept the inferno and become part of it that you can no longer see it. The second is risky and demands constant vigilance and apprehension. Seek and learn to recognize who and what, in the midst of the inferno, are not the inferno, then make them endure, give them space." ITALO CALVINO, *Invisible Cities.*

Although the work is imagistic it is not conceived by means of an advertising style story-board. Morphosis has held to a Vitruvian architecture with solid joints and supporting columns, albeit with frequent devices introduced to undo simple readings in terms of post-lintel structures. This gives the work the property Mayne refers to as an "idealized contingent language," combining idealized geometries and proportioning systems with remnants of contingent reality—an emphasis on unpredictable contrasts, changing focal distances, and incorporation of the details of ordinary life.

The unorthodox view finds meanings in the details of the descriptive surface. Vermeer's woman by the window reading a letter may not be spiritually absorbed (Annunciation images, for example) but may just as likely to be thinking about her extra-marital affair. There is no hard and fast distinction between primary surfaces and secondary "forms." Attention is given to the changing bricolage of expendable styles of clothing, music and other details of the "popular culture."

A movie location takes readings from diverse media, employing their mutual effects to generate a coherent experience. Odd details can be edited to the point of making their origins unrecognizable. For example, footrests and coat racks in Kate Mantilini bear a family resemblance to one another, vaguely like bulls horns made of tubular metal. They are mentally fused such that the original sources have long been forgotten. A new set of forms and functions have been defined by extending the program for this environment. Morphosis uses elements of a film aesthetic while adventurously "fishing" for elements in the surrounding junk heap of culture to use as the basis for inventing these new plastic forms. There are strains of both Charles Eames' fascination with Sweet's catalog and the ruminative quality of Piranesi's architectural autopsy (Tafuri, *Architecture & Utopia*) which transformed elements of the past into modern images. But the editing of the original source is so complete as to give the final products a distinctly "fetishistic" quality.

Current society is comprised of many subgroups, each with ethnic memories and traditions that have been diluted by the background mixing medium of bland corporate reality. Historically, there were a plethora of powerful architectural languages through which people and their struggles were represented. Classical Greek culture was used to justify a view of other languages as "inferior" and our own as privileged. This "monoglossia" bears much in common with the Spanish Inquisition in striking out the "patois" of varied forms of vernacular discourse. The problem is how to create a "coat of many colors" without giving privileged status to a single culture as the source. This reexamination of architectural sources explores the limits of "heteroglossia" (Bakhtin *Rabelais and His World*). Inevitably, it sanctions languages of the unofficial culture, amounting to their "carnivalization" (Jackson, "Street Life") in which popular culture transforms social relations of power by forcing out of the "wings" and on to the stage the peripheral images previously considered unsuitable for public view.

Note the potential of "rap" music to suspend the temporal and spatial order of the dominant culture. The music appropriates "street life" as its "genius loci." The stories are like those of classical troubadors, of people and their "trials," their struggles with temptation.

"You go to a club to chill out,
not to see someone's guts spill out."
RECORDING FROM STOP THE VIOLENCE MOVEMENT, "SELF-DESTRUCTION."

Early Morphosis projects are a prophetically short distance from the "carnival" atmosphere of Venice beach, an area with unique status in the LA region as a metaphor for the breakdown of distinctions of class. Even those with money and privilege identify with this turf. In the modern world they do not feel protected by wealth, for example, from the ravages of cancer due to effluents of industry. There is an analogy between the teratogenic process of cancer and the reediting mode of current art media. In both, there are no fixed elements. All processes of change are potentially "mutative." Objects can be digitally disassembled, split into multiple channels, stretched and compressed to make their origins unrecognizable.

19

The phenomenological program

The designs of Morphosis are answerable to users. The "phenomenological program" is a structurally coherent narrative text that defines the building and the forces that motivated it. The "phenomenological program" is something which resists being pictured. The buildings come together "poemically." The physical ingredients of a building create communication between architect and user, the way an engagement ring is more than a thoughtful gesture, stared at as if the lover is peering out of it.

It is not the conceptually sublimated, ironic evaluation of forms to be found in Jenck's notions of post-modernism (Jencks, *The Language of Post-Modern Architecture*). The phenomenological program we have in mind is suited to the fictive character of the contemporary mind which constructs its own mythologies by exchanges with the social and physical world. Conceived in this mode buildings are pieces of reality which serve as material for the contemporary "novel." They are no longer simple geometrical forms to which associative meanings have been attached. The meaning of an object grows out of the complex human social encounters in which it attains significance. For a carpenter, a door may be a finished piece of wood. In the context of the emotional texture of Raskolnikov's rooming house, the door becomes suffused with his ambivalence.

According to Geertz (*Interpretation of Cultures*), in order to make a context intelligible, it must be "thickly" described. Gestures have to be interpreted in terms of the meanings they have for the person as a member of a culture. A woman sitting on a rock with chin resting on her hand can be "simply resting" or "pretending to look deep in thought," "or parodying someone looking deep in thought." The issue is not so much the ontological status of the gesture, whether it is ultimately subjective or objective, mental or physical. Geertz accepts these things as being "of the world." The question then is to ask about their import: what it is that is getting "said" in their occurrence!

Comprehensive Cancer Center (CCC)

The key to the "phenomenological program" of the Comprehensive Cancer Center (CCC) stems from inherent contradictions in its form. This is an environment for people with a life threatening illness for whom there can be no moments of genuine rest. Even the most innocent settings are likely to evoke painful reminders of the mutagenic process.

The most humane act might be to build an environment which acknowledges the indeterminacy the patients face by veiling harsh distinctions, creating the equivalent of a domestic living room which offers temporary certainty. By contrast, the CCC is a tough environment which refuses to accept as contradictory the disease threat and the need to carry on the order of daily life.

The street level portion of the CCC is wedged into a thin portico with most of the development occurring below grade due to site constraints. It suggests a metaphorical crypt or grave, an anathema to patients en route to the clinic to get suffused with chemicals with massive toxic side effects.

Horizontality is the domain of the "facing" relation in which the child first experiences the loving illumination of the face of the mother. For depressed people, the sea (or a lake) is soothing because it helps them to recover this feeling of horizontality. The open expanse reminds them of the loving "face-to-face" orientation of caretaker and child. The horizon produces the contrasting feelings of majesty and insignificance, power and total surrender, all a return to the secure innocence of childhood. Loss of horizon translates metaphorically into a lack of mutuality, a breakdown in the sense of scale and proportion that comes out of contact with the social world. In psychotic depression, the hands wring together, the eyes are cast downward, and there is rejection of all horizontal overtures. It is a world without sunshine, of dark unlit dreams, power and punishment.

By contrast, vertical organization of the environment translates metaphorically into the concentration of energy. Vertical buildings organize possibilities of the situation around a small area and resist exterior influences, where horizontally organized buildings are accommodating of their environments. As we move upward in the vertical dimension we no longer "have our feet on the ground," and can either drift into fantasy detachment from the world, or in the extreme become psychotically detached.

There is a duality about the vertical dimension: the experience of "highs" (often associated with test of balance, a feeling of invulnerability to the weaknesses of the flesh) to a moribund "low" feeling that comes from entering below the plane of everyday reality. Moving downward in the vertical dimension connotes yielding to demands of the natural world. Sages in Chinese scroll art are drawn deeply sunken in the landscape as a symbol of mental tranquility or a surrender of resistance.

Users of the CCC already feel like "outsiders" (cf. WILSON, The Outsider), no way around or through, forced to endure the anxiety of entering. The building is approached with ambivalence, at once a place of refuge from illness, and at the same time a source of dread, shame and guilt. The building space begins at the first moment the person sees it from the parking lot. From there to the moment the electric doors glide open the plane of entry is charged with horizontal energy. Inside, the sliver wall comes to a reverse razors edge, symbolically shaving against the users' direction of flow, heightening awareness of their own motion. The canted reception desk projects into this plane, checking the rhythm but allowing the horizontal line of action to continue past it.

Most hospital lobbies project the patient instantly into an abstractly structured realm. They confront a reception desk, are placed in a wheelchair, elevatored up, down, around corridors, with little concern for their residual phenomenological experience. The body becomes a physical projectile (not flesh and blood) to be relocated in space. CCC uses the compressed entry level to channel the patients' motion, helping them recognize their capacity for "straight visual penetration." Focused vision gives them increased confidence in their ability to maintain balance, to keep oriented actively toward the world, thereby avoiding obsessive preoccupations that can come with the disease (even leading to psychosis).

The "freeze-dried tree" continues the datum line of the street outside. Two stories below in the waiting room a sculptural form lofts the tree upward (arguably a combination of spaceship gantry, X-ray machine, and planetary telescope), establishing a relationship with the lower area accessed by the elevator. This is the last clear moment of contact with the outside horizon.

"To be faced by nothing is to lose all measure, to be supported by nothing and to have nowhere to go."
STRAUS, Phenomenological Psychology

Once the patient has arrived at the treatment level, gateways (counters, windows and other frames) offer a phenomenological "facing" role to provide the patient with a sense of orientation. In its lower reaches, the environment becomes a place of spartan words and diminished gestures. Vertical descent is passage to a realm of contemplation in which the reaching hands and exploring eyes appropriate to coping with the outside world are gradually surrendered in a process analogous to dark adaptation. The patients give up worldly coping skills and turn with meditative awareness to their own internal physical processes.

In the treatment atrium itself, patients are alone in a three-sided niche with one side left open to the "barrel vaulted" common space. Provision is made for them to maintain indirect contact with the world (e.g., looking up through high windows) but not in the directed, "piercing" manner that is common in everyday reality. The effulgent daylight prevents the sense of interrogation that comes with artificially lit, bright spaces, as if all parts of the body are suspect. In their niche-like environments, the patients feel they have "backing." The enclosures provide a sense of support because they feel carved out of the subterranean strata that surround the structure.

Although drawn downward into a contemplative vertical realm they do not experience themselves to be locked inside. They are free to venture out to the open atrium in which a high-rise fish tank reinforces the idea of a new subterranean horizon. The architectural setting strikes a balance between enclosing concentration and despairing isolation. This is a piece of crafted fiction carefully keyed to the process of entering and using the building. Studied use of sectional and elevational data produces an environment which is simultaneously experienced in the vertical and horizontal dimensions. As one descends there is a growing sense of self-reflection and detachment from the everyday plane of reality. Plan organization provides the patient with the feeling of "backing" and "support" and both are integrated in the sectional unfolding of space.

21

Venice Alley Houses

Venice III is a project that compresses the cycles of daily life into a horizontally layered, multilevel vertical space. Being alone in the alley addition is a little like entering the twilight land between waking and sleep. In hypnogogic imagery the ego is lulled into allowing forbidden fantasies to merge with perceptions of docile reality. Like the "eyes open" process of free association on the analysts couch, ordinary reality becomes mixed in with unconscious reverie. The resulting emotions can be intense, even disturbing.

Unlike Morphosis' other projects, there is no distinct entry point to this small addition. The building sits on the alley behind a weathered Cape Cod house. Slipping inside through a small door, we find ourselves in the center of an inwardly focused "pantheonic space" which leaves the context behind. The eye is immediately drawn upward to survey multiple levels compressed into the small volume. There is also the visual task of solving the mystery of the internal surfaces, that is, the layering of screen walls, openings, connections and transparencies.

The piano nobile, hardly grand in scale, is established as continuous with the exterior grounds made visible through the reverse clerestory opening beneath the "floating bookcase." This begins to suggest the playful reversals that will occur later in the game. The added "glass to glass" corner next to the bookcase exposes the continuous surface of the grassy side and rear yards, strengthening the suggestion that the land on which the addition sits extends horizontally in all directions.

Climbing the stairs from this base level is audibly rhythmic, charged with visual significance by the discontinuous industrial roll stock perforated metal stair treads that sit on structural rods extending from the wall with no risers linking them with one another. It resembles the discontinuous stepping stones of a pilgrimage walk to a small mountain temple, or the unadorned armature of a lighthouse ladder. At the first landing, the bathroom is placed ironically in the three dimensional center of the space on a major axis like the Tomb of Cheops suspended in the Great Pyramid . The ascent continues on conventional stairs to the extended bedroom level, and eventually the

roof. Carefully framed views at each station establish a chain of connected, inhabited spaces. Each establishes a unique facing relation to the exterior. Each contrasts with the inward orientation of the building as a whole. Perhaps they become alternative orientations toward the self, diverse ways of relating "towards" that which is "beyond." The rectangular bedroom window offers a wide horizon, like the sense of measured social contact one feels when looking at the scattered arrangement of tiled houses of an Italian hillside. An overview of the varied Venice roofscape provides the same sense of warmth and compassion.

The living room is the ground plane, its form is a distorted evocation of the square, a symbol of geographical orientation based on the cardinal axes. The study is slotted beneath the ground plane creating a feeling of compression beneath the surface, burying within the landscape as a means of achieving contemplative tranquility, perhaps also symbolizing the binding oppression of an academic discipline.

It is a house for an intellectual, a classicist with love for removing herself from the present world to experience the discipline of an ancient era. This piece responds to a life of the mind. Sometimes this lifestyle requires forced isolation. Compulsive intellectuals can console themselves by means of control and mastery while shutting themselves off from worldly reciprocity. Or alternatively, as in the notion of the "ivory tower" the subject can lose a sense of proportion, assume a "commanding view," often suffering from flight between extremes, at one moment feeling they possess Archimedean power while moments later falling from grace to return to ordinary reality and suffering a loss of perspective. Then there is the stitching together of formal and informal elements into a misshapen whole. The body can be seen as both beautiful and grotesque. The classical lines of Greek statuary have little to do with the mortal facts of life. Classical buildings are complete unto themselves whereas contemporary buildings tend to overflow their limits. In relation to the body, the focus on food and evacuation, sex and birth, is a metaphorical confrontation with impulses. The body outgrows its limits and conceives a new second body in the bowels and the phallus. It breaches the boundary between its own and that of other bodies.

The grotesque image defies the closed, smooth, impenetrable surfaces of modern objects and allows for protuberances and bulges, holes and orifices. In so doing, it points to gaps in the completeness of the Apollonian logic employed by the dominant society. The purpose of irony is to expose the open endedness of hermetically sealed systems. All the "alley projects" distort the perfect cube by combining it with a bulging, skewed topiary wall. This small gesture challenges the discipline of ordinary suburban houses. Like Gehry's own house, the Mosk residence, or Eric Owen Moss's Petal House, the houses are forced out of their conventional boundaries to give birth to a new set of carnivalized forms. The 2-4-6-8 house stays close to the Bauhaus discipline of the cube. The minimalist challenge relates to the odd placement of the door, the arbitrary geometry, the cranks for air, electric shades hidden inside the brows over windows that are reminiscent of Jefferson's love of "tinkering." The Platonic form is modified to adapt it to contingent characteristics of the environment in which it sits.

Sedlak goes a step further in making the allegory of the house more complex. It integrates the thick, battered, occupied topiary wall with the geometric form of the cube. Now bathroom and desk find their way into odd shaped leftover niches created in the poched addition, like the insert in an orthopedic shoe. This cleavage between the topiary wall and the house/cube has analogous effects. Like adding a small limp to a natural gait, it changes the appearance of walking. Nonetheless, the total form has its own dance-like rhythms!

Venice III synthesizes these forms in a new whole. Platonic cube and eccentric elements have merged to create a new dynamic object that has elements of both the ordered and the unpredictable. The poched piece is now a wall filled with books—the library. The order of the universe is reversed in the three-dimensional space. The focus point is the philosopher's study. Rather than place it in a tower (itself an excrescence from the body of the house) it is imprisoned beneath the floor in a niche five steps down, with an eye level view of the rear garden lawn. It is this same downward motion that we find in the CCC. While it represents a retreat from the real world, it is not a stepping up and out of the present to join the Empyrean realm of the Classic Gods. Rather, it is a means of moving deeper into self reflection to decipher the meaning of classic forms in relation to contemporary times. (This is what I.F. Stone has done in the The Trial of Socrates).

72 Market

We have talked of a concern with extending beyond the corporeal limits of the box, stitching together an object from incoherent pieces, exhuming from the subsurface or substructure of ordinary reality a previously unrevealed seed of new life.

72 Market can be seen as a study in creativity and rebirth, exploring the dynamics of repressed aggression. The theme of the architectural intervention is a box, slightly rotated, within a regular rectangular volume (originally Robert Irwin's studio on Market Street in Venice). The canting of the "box" and access to it via a ramp motivates analogies to a womb and metaphors of rebirth.

Every artistic act is about rebirth and projects onto the world its own fantasy resolution of internal psychological conflicts. These adjustments are so fused with program, form and metaphor as to make their emotional sources unrecognizable.

This environment was commissioned by motion picture producer Tony Bill as a place for creative people in the movie business. Creativity involves the ability to exceed the limits of the material world, and, often as not, is rooted in aggressive fantasies of limitless expansion based on fracturing and fragmenting current reality. When this process fails to produce valued objects (like the unproductive artist) there is great guilt and remorse related to the scattering of seed; the loss of resources.

The architect similarly invests emotions in providing coherence to a set of parts which have no "natural" order. Failure results in guilt because artistic activity resembles "anal scattering" of random play. Adoption of an overly critical supervising ego (represented by the critical mother, or the studio "crit") can inhibit creativity by asserting that all products fall short of having the needed discipline. On the other hand, easy license encourages artistic narcissism, that is assuming any and all products are equally valuable. This narcissistic preoccupation is common in many of the arts.

23

The metaphor of 72 Market is related to the society of people who inhabit it. The internal box is a rigid seismic frame designed to prevent the literal "scattering" of the building in the event of a major earthquake. It offers a grim reminder of the risks of fragmentation that can occur at any moment in time, either due to a physical event or a psychological breakdown.

There is a wonderful play between the classicized order of the interior and the carnival environment of the Venice boardwalk just one half block away. Venice is the realm of flotsam and jetsam "outsiders" to the society at large. Movie moguls thrive on obtaining access to the disorder of the streets as a source of energy. They risk being trapped in a dead inner world that signifies creative sterility. But then there is the concomitant fear of disorder, the disgust and shame that comes from contact with the expelled, scattered inchoate products of human activity, the decay, health deficiencies and crude bodily needs of the homeless.

The restaurant "parti" is a formal exercise in the Corbusian sense of evoking harmonious proportions. In another way it is an exploration of the phenomenological transgression of exterior and interior where the two are not in harmony (as for example La Tourette relates to the countryside). Eroding copper and concrete surfaces on the exterior become more elegant and refined on the controlled interior. They are part of a continuous physical reality, but that is as far as their similarity extends. This is appropriate for a social system with the contradictions of million dollar condos next to food kitchens for the homeless.

Kate Mantilini

In the case of Kate Mantilini, the context is the fast moving streetscape of Wilshire Boulevard and Beverly Hills. The space has been compressed to create a streetside dining terrace on the long south facing facade. The rhythm set up by the series of glazed interior booths and outside counters gives this elevation an elegantly spartan Miesian geometry.

The poched battered wall is now inside the building, the booths carved into its lower thickened portion. The metaphor of the topiary wall now faces inward to an enclosed, controlled garden-like space. The metaphor is underlined by the cracked stucco on its upper expanses.

The most profound orienting device is the "orrery," part mural, part working model of the universe with its evocations of astronomical observatory. The round domical form above establishes a vertical thrust and creates an unconscious equation with the coordinated phenomenology of section and plan that occurs in the great cathedrals of Europe. Nave and side-aisles, altar and dome are evoked, albeit in a distorted sequence, by the juxtaposition of elements.

At the base of the "orrery" the creative process of building has been recorded as a piece of the architectural plans, its hieroglyphic "genetic code" is inscribed in the floor. The concept of the "orrery" dates to the work of David Rittenhouse, a contemporary of Thomas Jefferson. It is emblematic of the faith both men had in Newtonian mechanics. They were intoxicated with the perfection of man-made designs, like the escapement mechanisms of clocks reflecting the harmonious movement of the universe. This is very similar to the enthusiasm current scholars have for the computer as a means of clarifying the operations of the mind. It was this aesthetic appreciation of mechanics of equilibrium that Jefferson attempted to infuse into the design of U.S. government. The "orrery" is an astonishingly modern idea, a mixture of scientific model and work of art.

The Morphosis "orrery" is frozen in motion, perhaps suggesting that models of the design process can not be reduced to axioms of science. Like old oil derricks or abandoned railway trestles, this "orrery" device reveals that the recording is either irrelevent, arrested or incomplete.

A chair for the Post-nuclear Club

Finally, this selective review will close with an analysis of a small item, among many that could be selected for intensive study, a chair designed originally for the "Post-nuclear Club." The chair can be described as an incomplete gesture inviting participation of the user to be mentally completed. The tapering half arm and back are fragments of the supporting gesture offered by (say) a "courthouse chair." To sit on it, however, requires a conscious adjustment of the act of sitting to accommodate the incompleteness of the object. The vestigial rear legs resemble an auto shock absorber that has been recast to create a visual diagram of the physics of sitting. The roll stock, rigid perforated metal seat has been arched to visually evoke the tufting and padding of an ordinary unholstered cushion which anticipates body contact.

There is a visual parable here about the change in status from chair as an object of contemplation to that of a "seat" with which one interacts. It is reminiscent of Aldo Van Eyck's distinction between a circle drawn with a compass and one drawn around the edge of a saucer. The concept of a "chair" is relevent only at moments when it has the status as an engineered object, e.g., in the furniture store at the moment of purchase. Seats on the other hand, are typically experienced with the eyes diverted, part of an intimate act that ends with intimate contact. The gesture of sitting is a kind of "backward dancing" keyed to the cues that are present in a familiar setting. In one's own home, as about to slip into the "easy chair," we are dancing toward certain, unencumbered contact, just as sure of the supportive response of the chair as one lover's response to the reaching gesture of the other. Backward movement is disagreeable in situations where it must be guided by optical sensations, like driving a car in reverse, i.e., where the body becomes a deliberate "tool" rather than an extension of its self.

The "I" of a person of action is located in the eyes. To know something is metaphorically equivalent to being able to "see it." When the "I" is shifted downward into the lower reaches of the torso, as in dance, the object is incorporated in the dramatic power of the gesture. There are cases of motor apraxia where the fluidity of this dance-like relationship of organism and environment can no longer be assumed (cf. OLIVER SACHS, *The Man Who Mistook His Wife For A Hat*).

Part of the message of the Morphosis chair is to question the fluidity of the everyday environment. If the conventions of the dominant culture are no longer unconscious, all our interactions with the world require intentional guidance. How can we establish fluidity and familiarity without using the corrupted conventions of the dominant culture? Is this not a reference to what has become of our cities? That a street once used unconsciously as a place of social contact, has been deprived of its intelligibility due to fear of crime, requires deliberate, conscious actions to use it safely!

The metaphor of "backward dancing" can also be used to refer to the narrative history of the culture. Historians who are part of the mainstream culture can mentally gesture backwards in time with comfortable familiarity. As history is increasingly subject to examination from the diverse perspectives of women, vernacular communities, and a variety of subcultures searching for their own identity, conditions arise which disrupt the fluidity of the historic act.

From its most complex programmatic work, such as the CCC, to the dimensioning and design of a simple chair, these architectural ensembles explore ethical dilemmas. They require the user to actively complete the forms rather than use them unconsciously. Le Corbusier assumed the only thing that was primitive about early cultures was the lack of resources and technology. Otherwise, all would have discovered the same Platonic universals that became accessible to the Greeks, and by lineage to western culture.

The alternative to this polemical view is a more radical "dialogic" conception of the social origins of architecture (Bahktin, *The Dialogic Imagination*). This view offers a refreshing alternative to the definition of the self "alone" which led romanticism into a solipsistic retreat from the social world. To take seriously the "dialogic" view means to take the self as whole only in relation to other "selves." The self is a collective project. In my perception of self I include the way I am perceived by the "other." We exchange the gift of perceptible self with one another. By analogy to the culture of architecture it suggests the importance of heteroglossia, incorporating in the view of one architecture culture, the works as they appear from the vantage of other cultures.

Bibliography:

BAKHTIN, *The Dialogic Imagination*, M.I.T. Press, 1981.
BAKHTIN, *Rabelais and His World*, M.I.T. Press, 1968.
CALVINO, *Invisible Cities*, Pan Books, 1979.
GEERTZ, *The Interpretation of Cultures: Selected Essays*, Basic Books, 1973.
JACKSON, "Street Life: The Politics of Carnival" in Environment and Planning D.: Society and Space, 1988, Vol. 6, pp. 213–227.
JENCKS, *The Language of Post-Modern Architecture*, Rizzoli, 1977.
LASSWELL, *The Signature of Power*, Transaction Books, 1970.
LEARS, "The Concept of Cultural Hegemony" in, American Historical Review, 90, pp. 567–593.
MERELMAN, *Making Something of Ourselves: On Culture and Politics in the United States*, University of California Press, 1984.
SACHS, *The Man Who Mistook His Wife for a Hat and Other Clinical Tales*, N.Y. Summit Books, 1985.
SONTAG, As Quoted in Jerzy Kosinski's *The Hermit of 69th Street: The Working Papers of Norbert Kosky*, Henry Holt & Company, 1988.
STRAUS, *Phenomenological Psychology: The Selected Papers of Erwin W. Straus*, N.Y. Basic Books, 1966.
TAFURI, *Architecture & Utopia: Design & Capitalist Development*, M.I.T. Press, 1976.
WILSON, *The Outsider*, V. Gollancz, 1958.

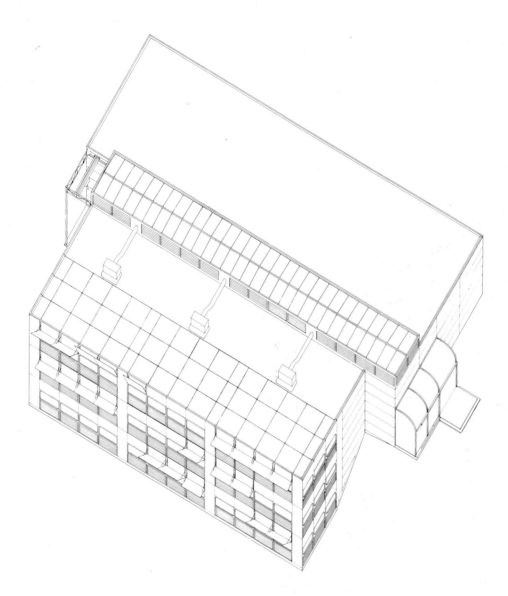

The Sequoyah Educational Research Center was designed to accommodate 200 students between the ages of 13 and 18, 25 faculty staff members and 10 to 15 researchers on a 450 acre ranch in the Santa Monica Mountains overlooking the Pacific Ocean. The facility was to have been built in two phases, the second phase consisting of an expansion of the research facilities and a summer education camp. The building was designed to be adaptable and to make efficient use of energy.

The core of the building is made up of administrative and faculty offices, conference areas, and an eating area. This was a to be a fixed structure with a movable interior. A multi-purpose area was connected to this core by a flexible spine and was to have had movable floor and wall panels. A gantry moved along the spine on a track on top of storage areas in order to serve the major public areas of the center. A completely demountable structure was to be used to construct movable instruction areas.

Sequoyah Educational And Research Center

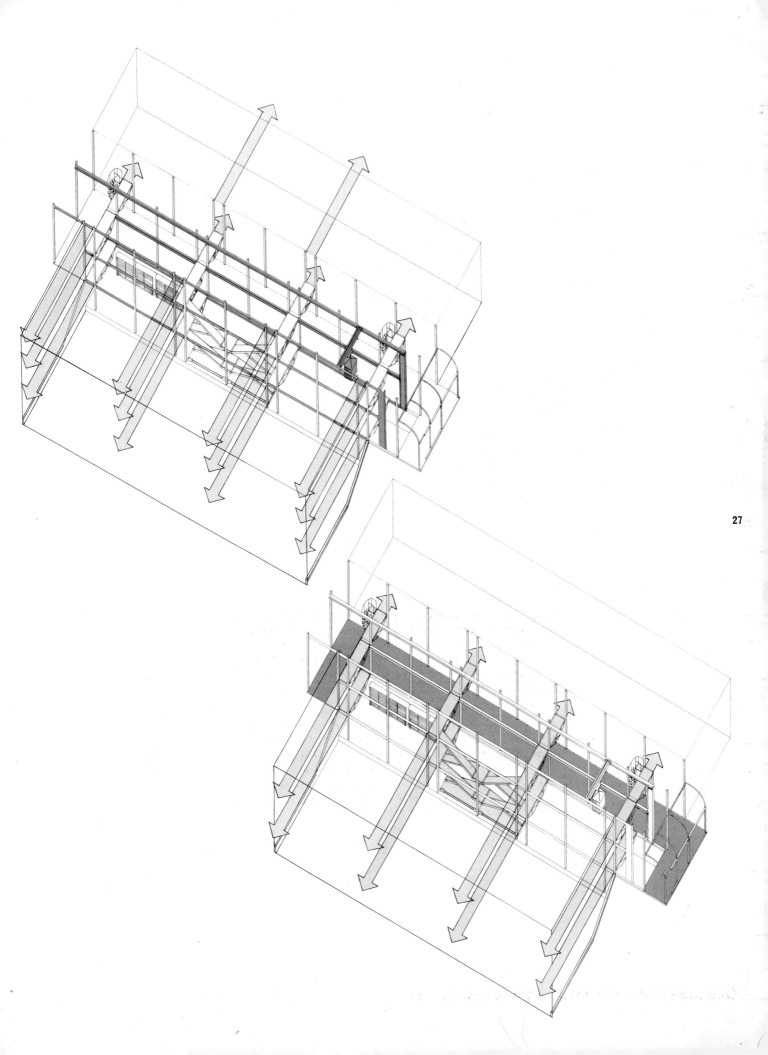

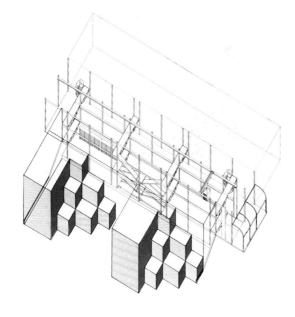
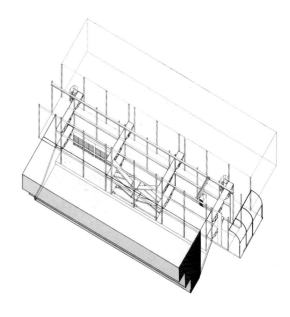

28

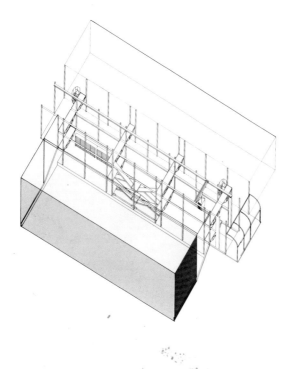
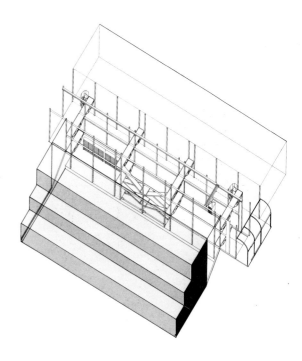

The building design makes use of interchangeable parts which would have allowed the building to adapt to changes in program and climate. These parts included structural scaffolding, mobile toilet units, plug-on mechanical systems, floor- and wall panels and furniture. By using this system, the educational facility could have been demounted, relocated and reassembled in any desired configuration. This operation would allow the building to make best use of the site and the climate at different times of the year. The solution exhibits the relationship between climate, site and construction as an extension of the didactic mission of the center, while the architecture is a means of adapting to environmental stress.

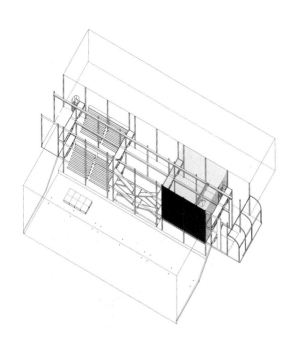

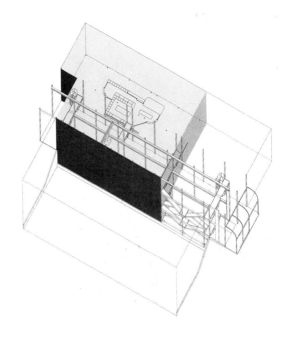

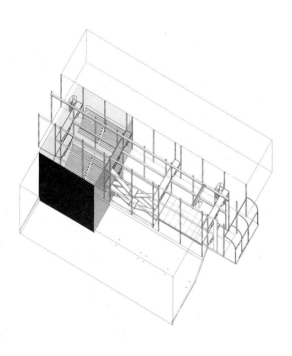

30

La Floresta Housing

Four prototypical single houses with three bedrooms and one-and-a-half baths and an area of 85 to 100 square meters were designed for an extremely low budget on 200 flat subdivided lots in Tijuana.

In order to maximize the small lots and be able to house large families while keeping within a tight budget, the lots were zoned for four specific activities: auto/entry court; living area; family courtyards; and service yards. The units themselves were then zoned into three distinct areas: living; sleeping; and linkage. This unit organization separated living from sleeping, thus maximizing privacy and creating the illusion of a larger unit.

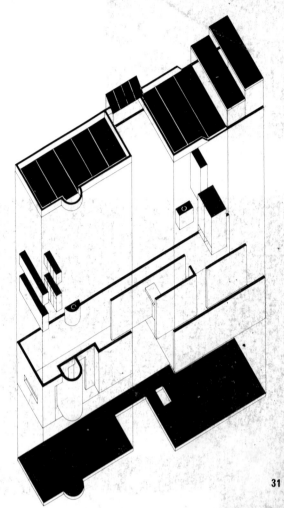

Four plans were developed to respond to varying family preferences and site conditions, but all units shared a common planning module employing dimensional coordination and allowing the use of repetitive spatial types. The bedroom zones in all units are identical, and utility cores, cabinets and other standard service elements are designed as modular components. The composition of these spaces and components was generated by a desire to both open up interior space through layering and to develop a common vocabulary through the expression of the basic building systems.

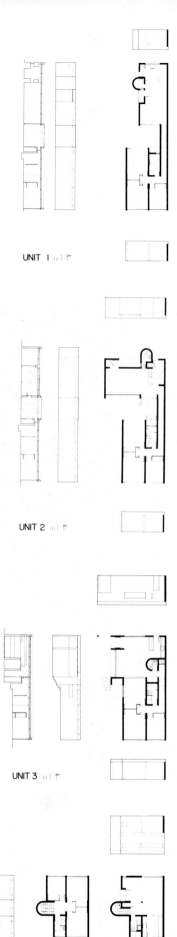

UNIT 1

UNIT 2

UNIT 3

UNIT 4

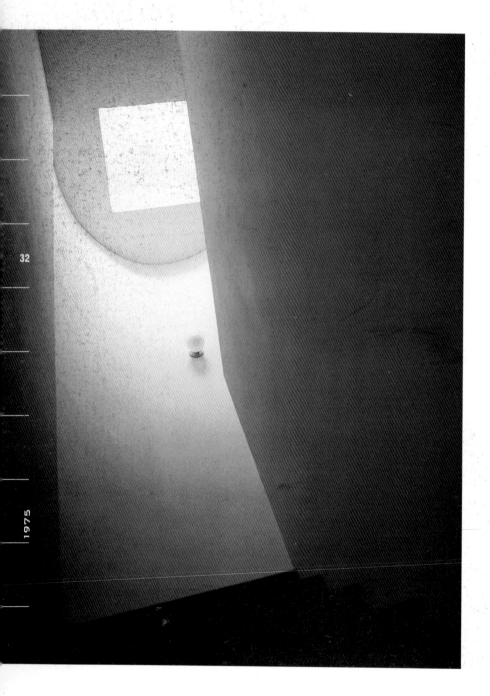

32

1975

Indigenous methods of construction and material were combined with more technologically advanced and quicker methods of assemblage. The walls were to have been made of concrete block covered with stucco on the outside and with plaster on the inside. The houses were to be built on concrete slabs on grade, covered with precast, prestressed concrete planks. Room partitions also served as storage cabinets in order to minimize the amount of walls, thus reducing the cost and expediting construction.

33

Reidel Medical Building

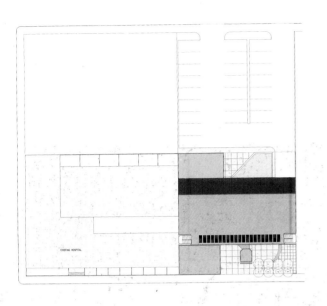

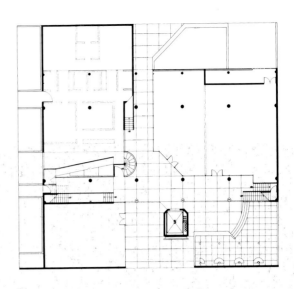

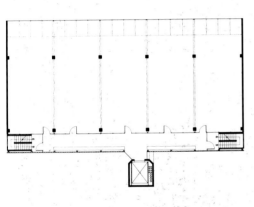

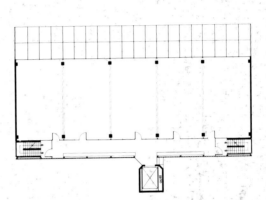

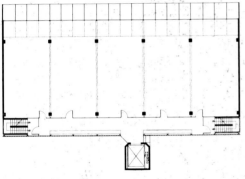

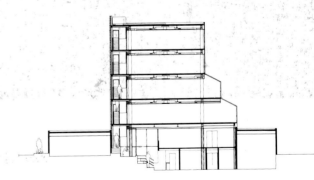

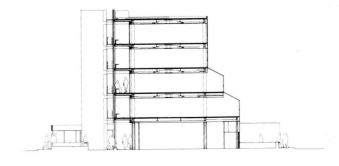

Set on a 1/2 acre site adjacent to a hospital in suburban Tijuana, Mexico, this building's 25,000 square feet are divided into three functional areas. The spine, which accommodates major circulation, also accomodates waiting spaces for patients' extended families. Oriented west, this environmental "bumper" is made of glass block to minimize solar penetration and heat gain. The commercial ground floor spaces are oriented towards the major street and to places of easy public and private access. The office block has five suites on each of four floors, with a varying building depth to allow for offices of three sizes. Horizontal organization is developed around fixed wet cores to allow for expansion of single offices into larger suites.

The building is designed with a sequence of transparent planes connected to the adjacent building by a space rather than by a solid. A glass block wall forms a skin that is separate from the circulation spine, resulting in one's simultaneous awareness of the horizontal and vertical space.

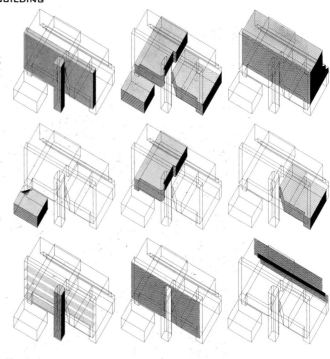

36

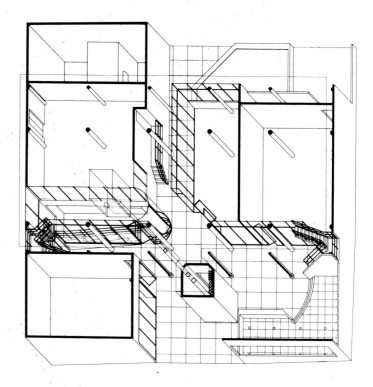

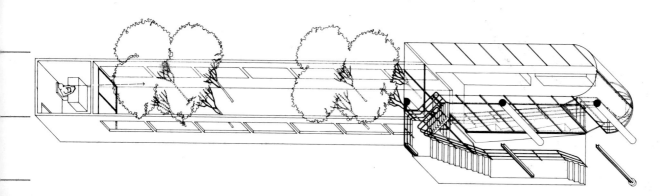

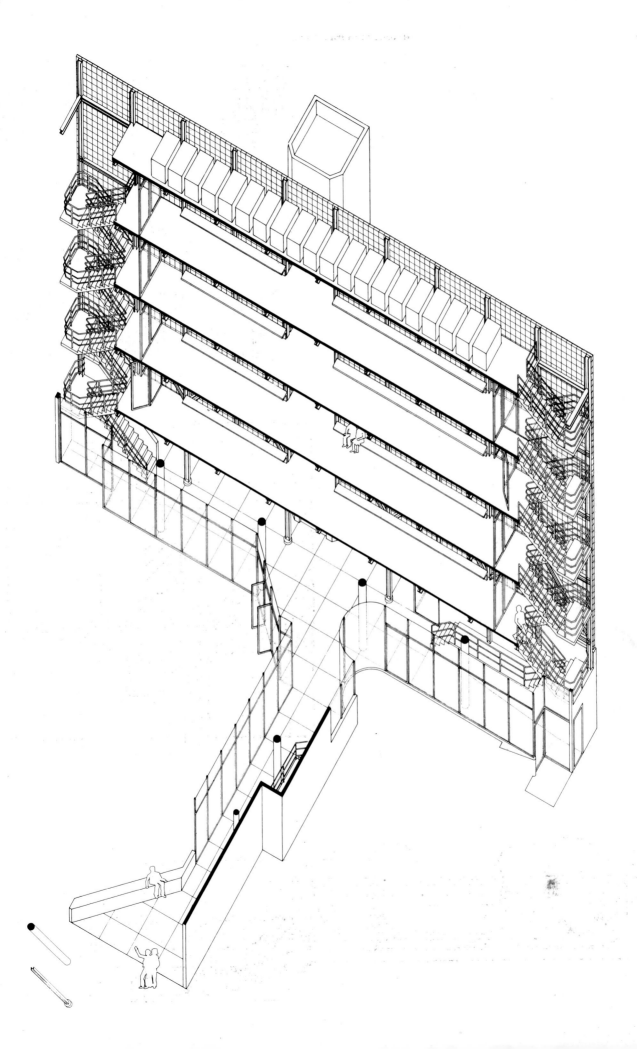

Delmer House Remodel

A sitting room/bedroom, master bathroom and roof deck were added to a cottage bungalow built in the 1920s. The deck provides for an ocean view and sunbathing. The addition extends the living space vertically onto a roof-deck, standing against the diversity of the beach community of Venice, California.

40

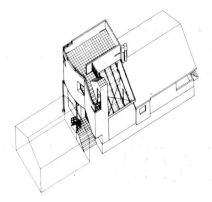
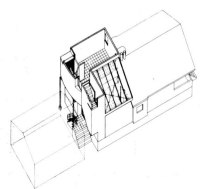
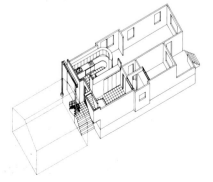

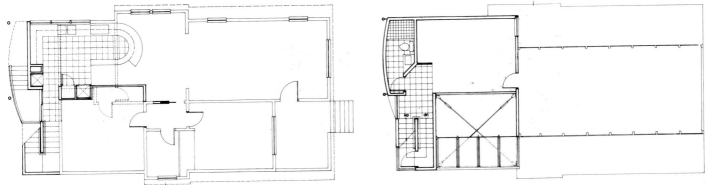

Sacramento State Office Building Competition

In response to a competition calling for an office building and housing in an area of lifeless, inactive streets which should be clearly and evidently energy conscious, we created buildings whose idealized shapes were acted upon by both real and conceptual forces. Energy was studied not as an isolated design determinant, but also both symbolically and in relationship to specific building requirements, the urban context and economic parameters.

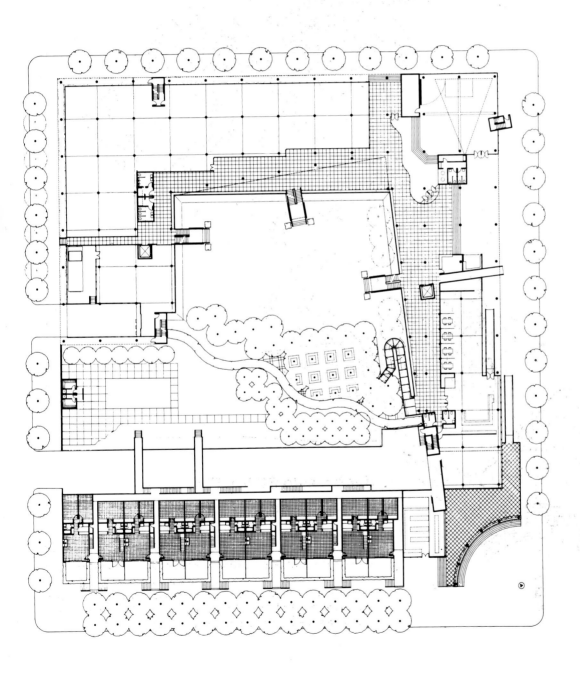

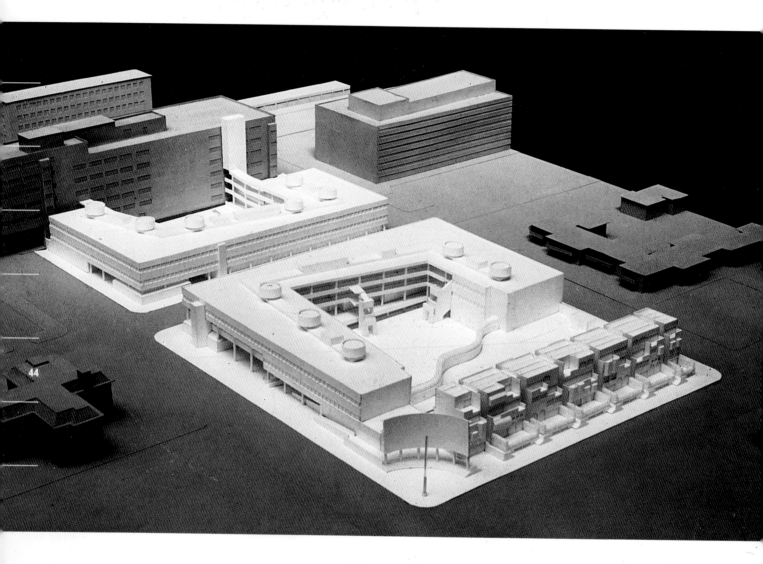

44

1977

The building fills the block and is organized around a courtyard. The offices line three sides of the interior garden or courtyard as slabs, thus identifying each of the separate departments housed in this complex. The housing is located on the north side of the complex to maximize sun and views. Each side of the block varies according to the needs of a complex program and the conditions of the street. One enters the complex through a corner entrance plaza which is made ceremonial in the manner of Stonehenge or Pueblo Bonita by a prism sculpture. This piece produces a color spectrum on a curved screen. One moves through the complex by using the courtyard or through four 12 foot wide stacked interior streets. The courtyard is organized around overscaled stairtowers which encourage use and dramatize the scale of this major public space. The walls of this garden space are cranked to the south to create a sense of space. Plantings here are formal and refer to the design of the nearby State Capitol.

In contrast to the smooth, mechanical images of the office complex, the housing was developed as a varied collage of images and styles characteristic of the individual use of these four-unit four-story urban villas.

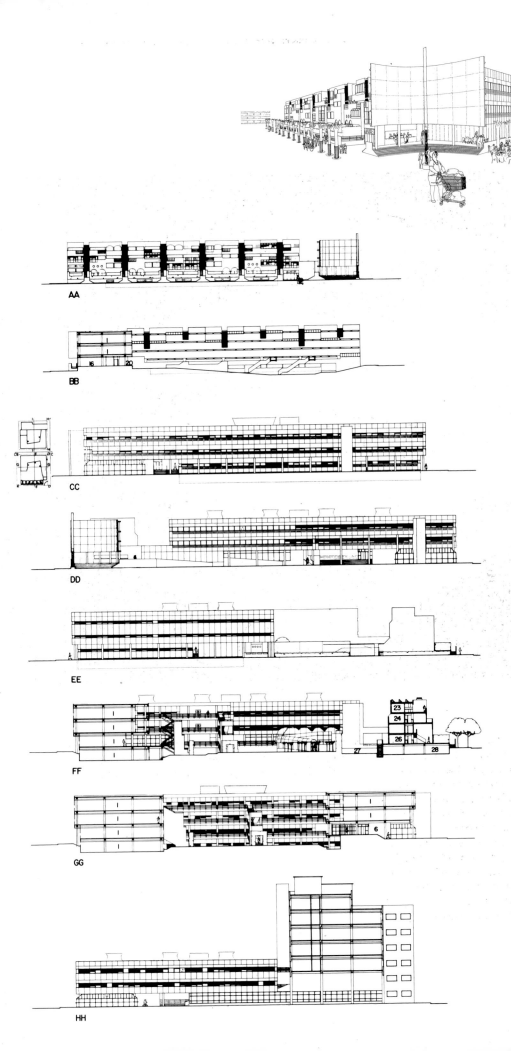

AA

BB

CC

DD

EE

FF

GG

HH

1978

Mexico House II

This house in Baja California is zoned into three areas: a garage and kitchen which flank the entry; a central living space used for entertaining and configured like the traditional thatched-roof *palapa* which are placed on the beach for festive occasions; and the bedrooms. Circulation, which is along the edges of these three zones, is conceptually exterior, as the zones are marked by continuous skylights and a topiary wall at the atrium space. The interior volumes are visually opened to each other in order to compensate for the small, 10 meter by 25 meter lot.

In the construction of the house, indigenous methods and materials, which made building the house easier, are combined with more technologically sophisticated and quicker methods of assembly. The walls are made of concrete block covered with stucco on the outside and with plaster on the inside. The foundations and the roof are concrete slabs, and the floors are covered with indigenous clay tile.

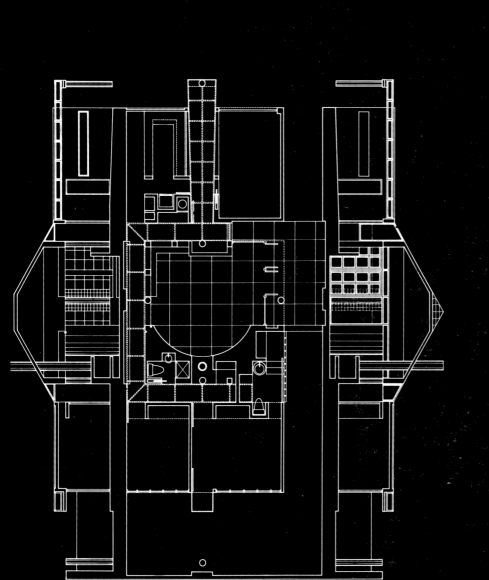

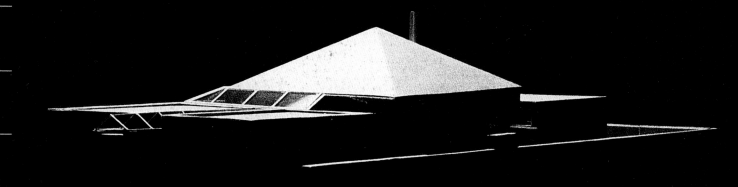

1978

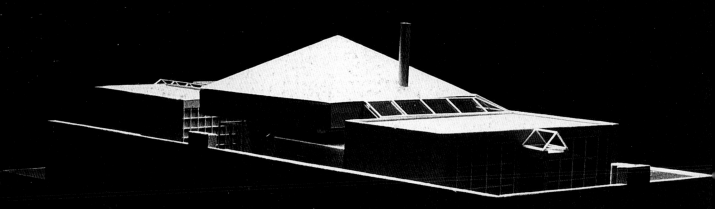

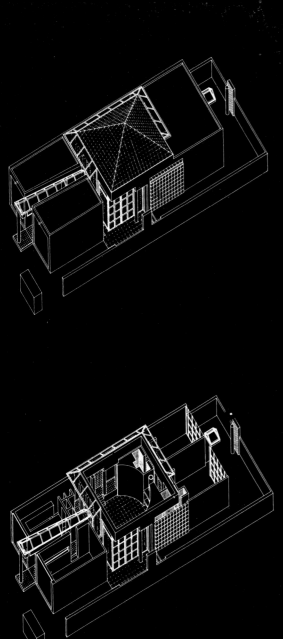

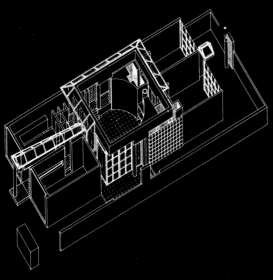

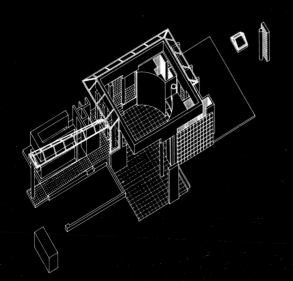

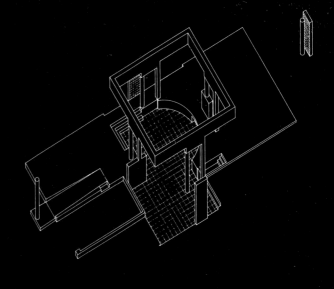

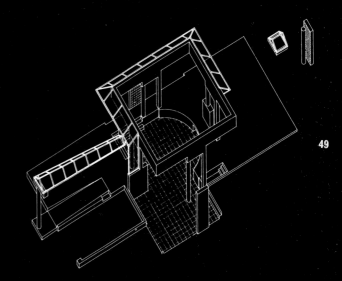

49

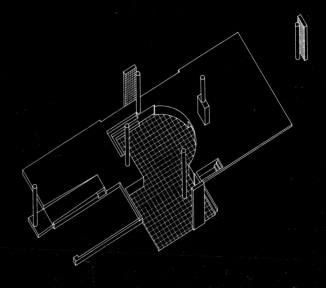

1978

2-4-6-8 House

Our client, who served as the builder of the project, desired a room for privacy and meditation which could function for a broad range of activities. This studio was to added onto a 1920s beach bungalow.

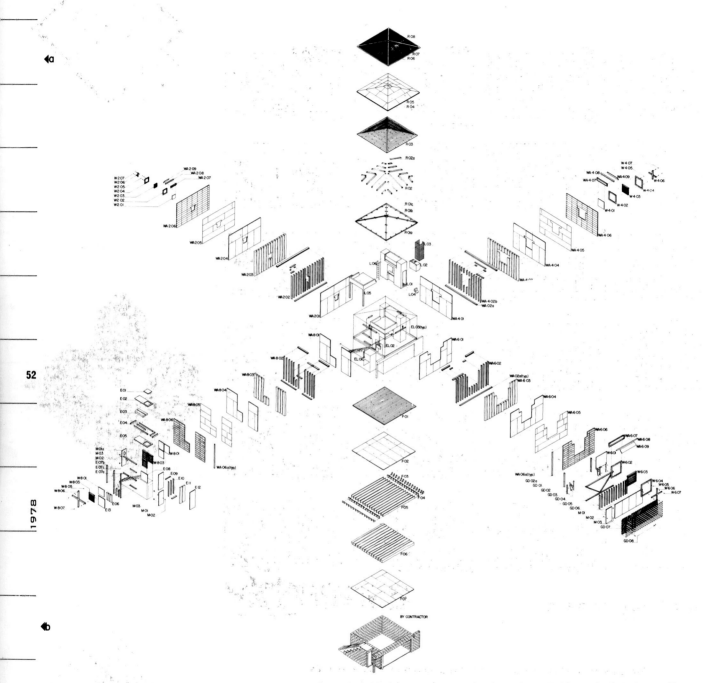

1978

2·4·6·8 HOUSE©   MOD. # MOR-746·747

parts
PRINTED IN USA

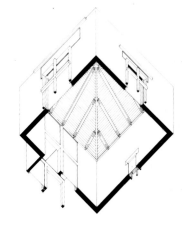

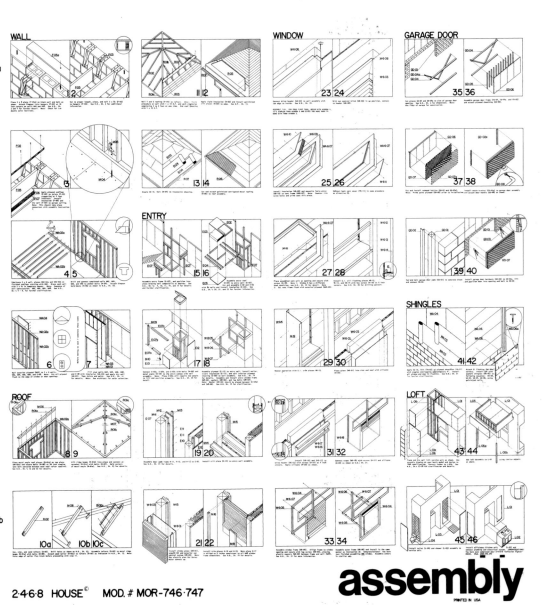

assembly

PRINTED IN USA

2·4·6·8 HOUSE© MOD. # MOR-746·747

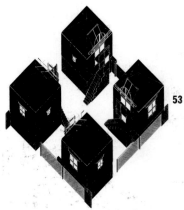

53

Because we wished to communicate with the client and were interested in the formal terms of the design of the house, we created a "Revell-like" kit. This kit documented the project in a familiar format that could be understood by a layperson and could help to alleviate some of the fear and confusion inherent in undertaking such a formidable task. The kit contained two posters which cataloged the building materials and described a basic step-by-step construction assembly. A pocket-sized set of working drawings served as the major means of communication with the client.

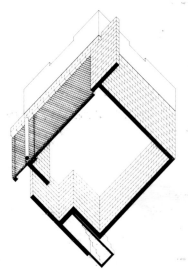

The primary design objective was to develop a simple, straightforward building that reflected the client's values. In order to reinforce the aspect of retreat, the studio was conceived of as a one-volume detached house placed over a two-car garage behind the existing residence. There are modest provisions for kitchen and bath. The house is of conventional wood balloon frame and is covered with asphalt shingles.

55

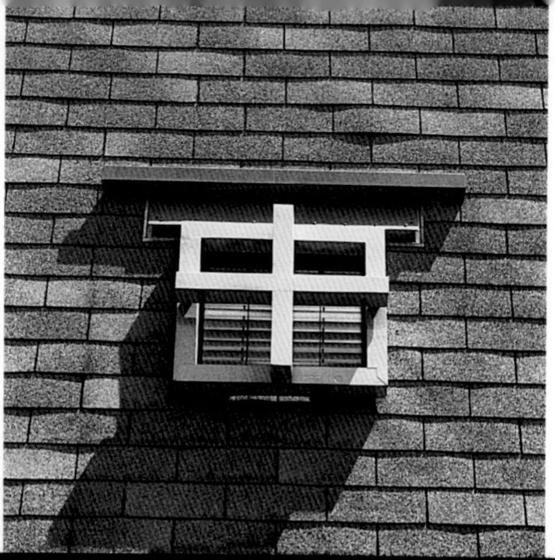

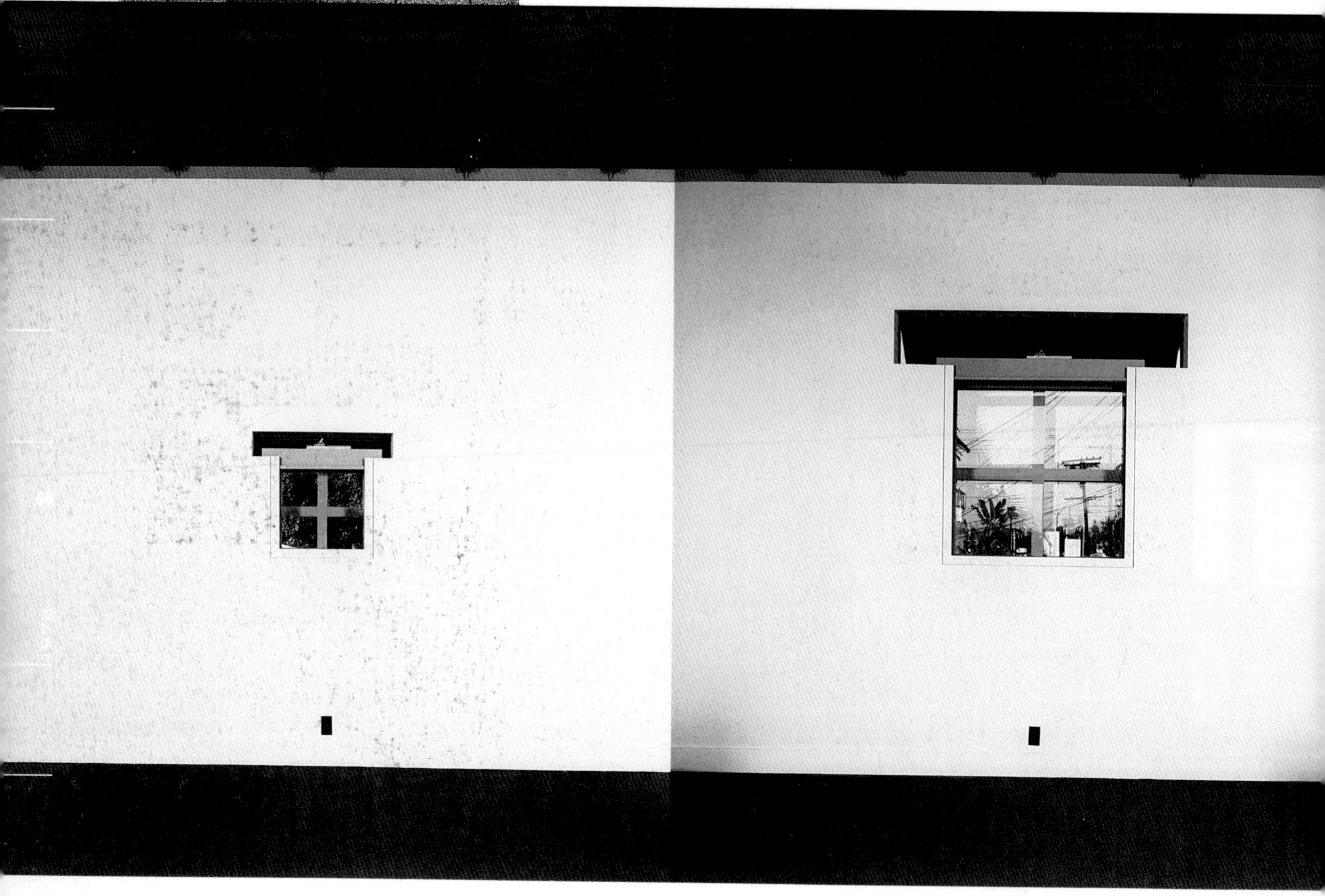

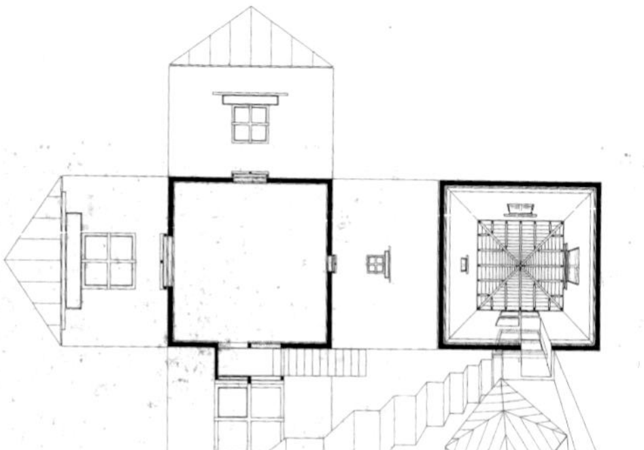

The windows were designed to reinforce the centrality of the space, while offering a differentiated perception of the external milieu. The building is neither heated nor cooled mechanically, it depends on the one "conventional" window for environmental control. The sunlight is controlled through external servo-operated blinds. The space is naturally ventilated by manually operated vents which project as lintels on three sides. Hot water is provided by solar collector panels. All of these parts are expressed as gadgets to be played with.

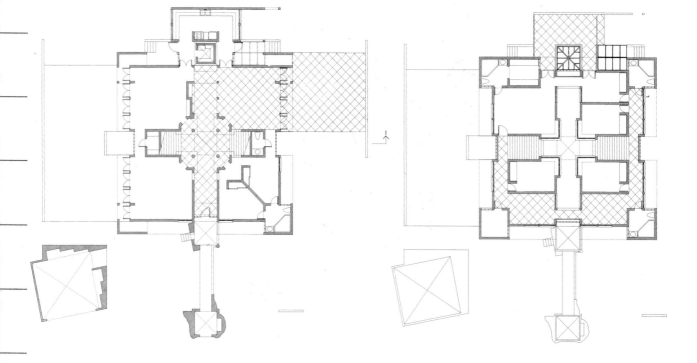

Modebe House

Our clients were a family of five who were returning home to Onitsha, Nigeria, after fourteen years abroad. They wished to live on a large parcel of land that had been family-owned as far as anyone could remember, with their three brothers, a nephew and the spirits of their fathers and ancestors. The house is also organized to accommodate other family members and guests who visit frequently.

Two significant factors emerged out of many client meetings. First, the building had to respond to the influence of two distinct cultures: Ibo and European. The house had to recognize the differences and commonality of both cultures and to reconcile the conflicts inherent in both. Second, the house had to be organized in a manner that restored the

type of social interaction that was particular to Ibo culture. In the traditional Ibo house immediate and extended family are allowed into all rooms without restriction, but friends and acquaintances have access only to a guest-family room and have to be invited into all other spaces. Visual and physical privacy are required by custom. This zoning was accomplished by creating detached buildings within a compound. The space between the buildings was the most public and was used for general activities.

Though this form of organization has been discarded, we have attempted to develop an architecture which alludes to the two cultures in its plan, formal vocabulary, and method of construction.

The house adheres to the principle of the compound, while its structure utilizes Cartesian geometry. Each quadrant within the latter order represents a distinct building, all of which are connected by an enclosed two-story space. The service areas are appended to the main body of the house and form secondary buildings. The house will be made of concrete block, wood, glass, glass block, tile and metal roof. The compound will be entered through a traditional portal gate leading into a reception building, which also serves as a porch.

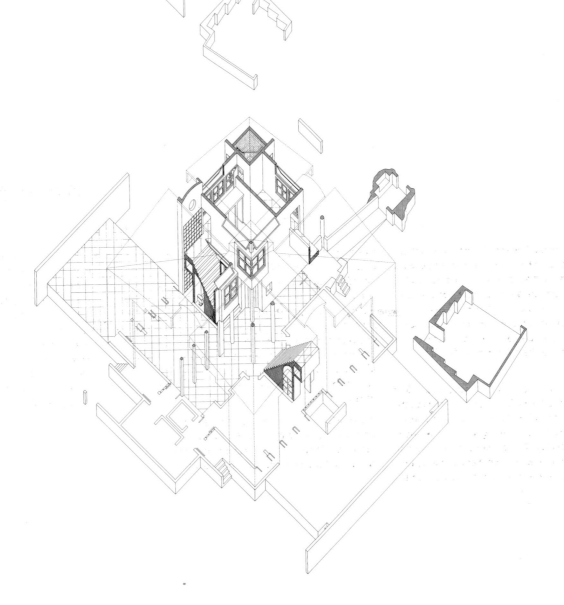

1979

**Flores
Residence
Addition**

A formal dining space, bedroom, bath, loft, utility room, carport and sundeck
were added onto a one-story "California 50s" house. The addition was
designed in a manner that would allow it to be perceived as being distinct
from the existing house. The expansion also reversed the sequence of movement from front to back to facilitate a new entrance while reinforcing the
existing north/south circulation axis.

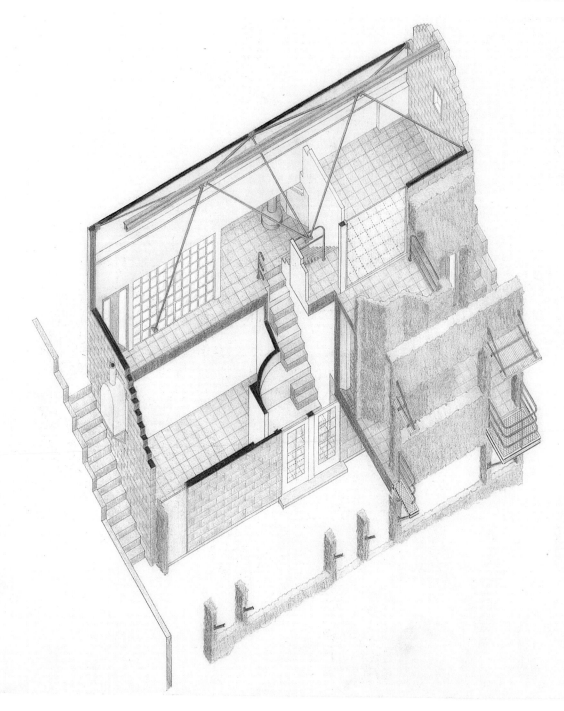

62

1979

The long, rectangular plan is surmounted by a 13 foot diameter barrel vault. The north/south walls which frame this sequence dissolve from plaster and glass block into a structural topiary supporting a topiary roof and finally become a free-standing green hedge wall. The topiary terminates the sequence and frames the distant ocean view. Beyond the topiary, a metal perch acts as an unconfined space lifted up beyond the hillside.

Just as the addition is distinct from the house, so the various components are independent: the wall does not quite engage the roof, the railing is separate from the hedge.

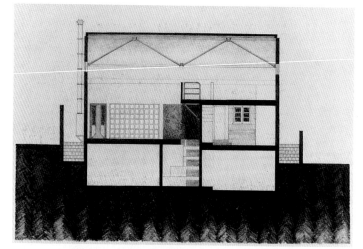

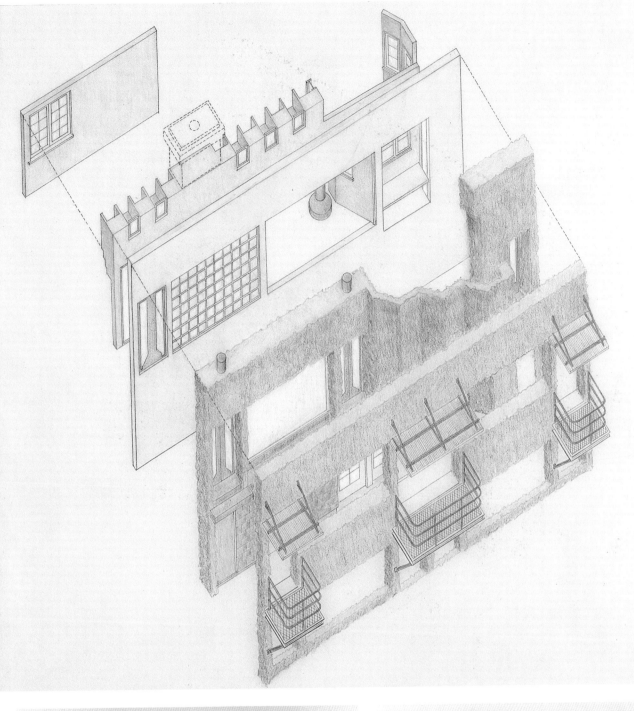

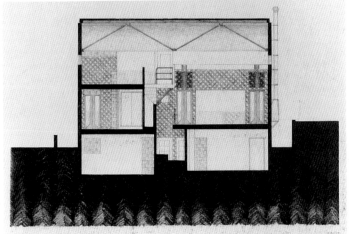

1979

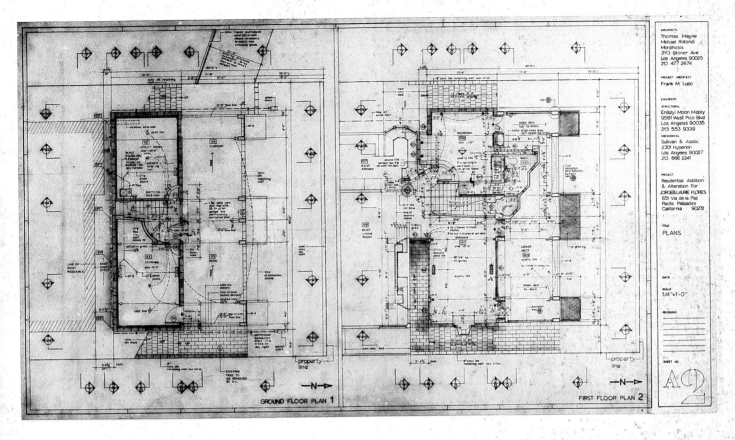

GROUND FLOOR PLAN **1**

FIRST FLOOR PLAN **2**

ARCHITECTS
Thomas Mayne
Michael Rotondi
Morphosis
2113 Stoner Ave
Los Angeles 90025
213 477 2674

PROJECT ARCHITECT
Frank M. Lupo

ENGINEERS

STRUCTURAL
Erdelyi Moon Mezey
9581 West Pico Blvd
Los Angeles 90035
213 553 9339

MECHANICAL
Sullivan & Assoc.
2301 Hyperion
Los Angeles 90027
213 668 2241

PROJECT
Residential Addition
& Alteration For
JORGE/LAURE FLORES
651 Via de la Paz
Pacific Palisades
California   90272

TITLE
PLANS

DATE

SCALE
1/4"=1'-0"

REVISIONS

SHEET NO.

A 2

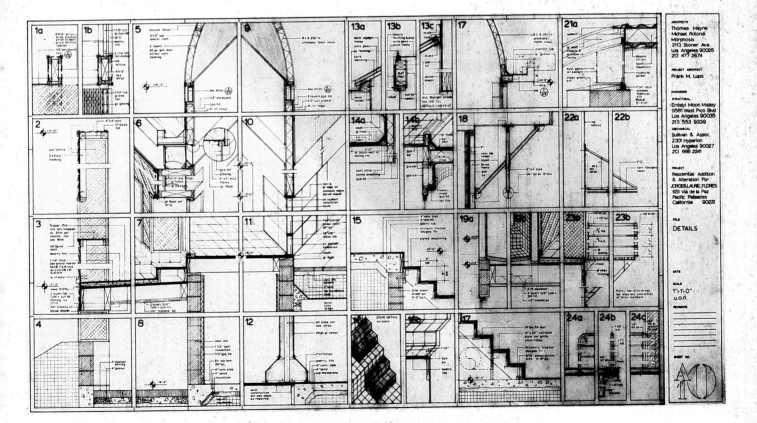

DETAILS

ARCHITECTS
Thomas Mayne
Michael Rotondi
Morphosis
2113 Stoner Ave
Los Angeles 90025
213 477 2674

PROJECT ARCHITECT
Frank M. Lupo

ENGINEERS

STRUCTURAL
Erdelyi Moon Mezey
9581 West Pico Blvd
Los Angeles 90035
213 553 9339

MECHANICAL
Sullivan & Assoc.
2301 Hyperion
Los Angeles 90027
213 668 2241

PROJECT
Residential Addition
& Alteration For
JORGE/LAURE FLORES
651 Via de la Paz
Pacific Palisades
California   90272

TITLE
DETAILS

DATE

SCALE
1"=1'-0"
u.o.n.

REVISIONS

SHEET NO.

A 10

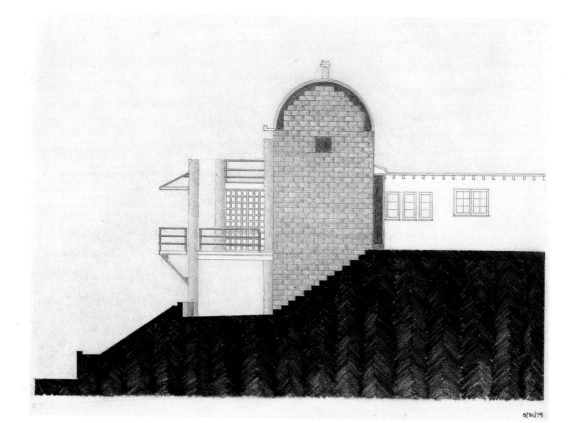

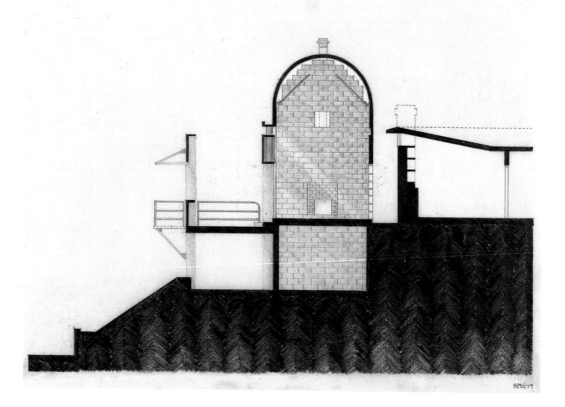

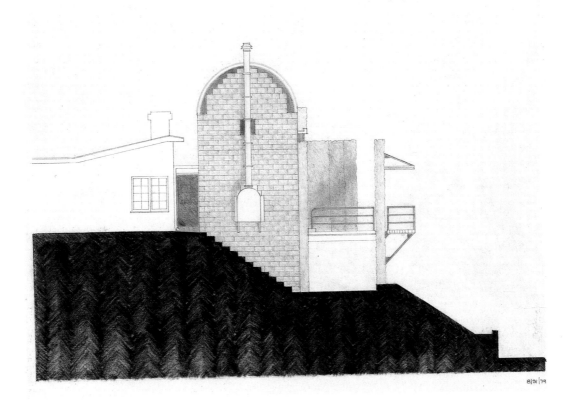

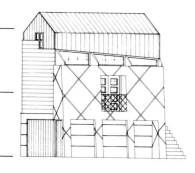
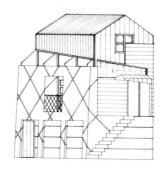

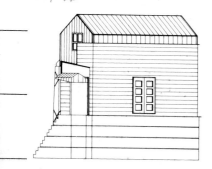

**Sedlak
Residence
Addition**

OCT 22 1979

This building is placed over a one-car garage to the rear of a single family residence and consists of a single room and study used as a retreat. We wished to minimize the impact of the new building's appropriation of a large part of the yard and allow a coherent, ideal object to emerge. To accomplish both of these goals, we created a topiary wall which camouflages the building and allows the idealized object to develop out of a contingent condition. We could then use the building to explore the relationship between architecture and landscape. The topiary wall is thick enough to make room for three small rooms that service the main space: a bathroom, a balcony and a desk alcove. An entry arcade at ground level leads to a stairway rising to the doorway. The materials refer to those already used on the site, and also describe the different parts of the building.

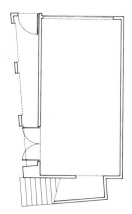

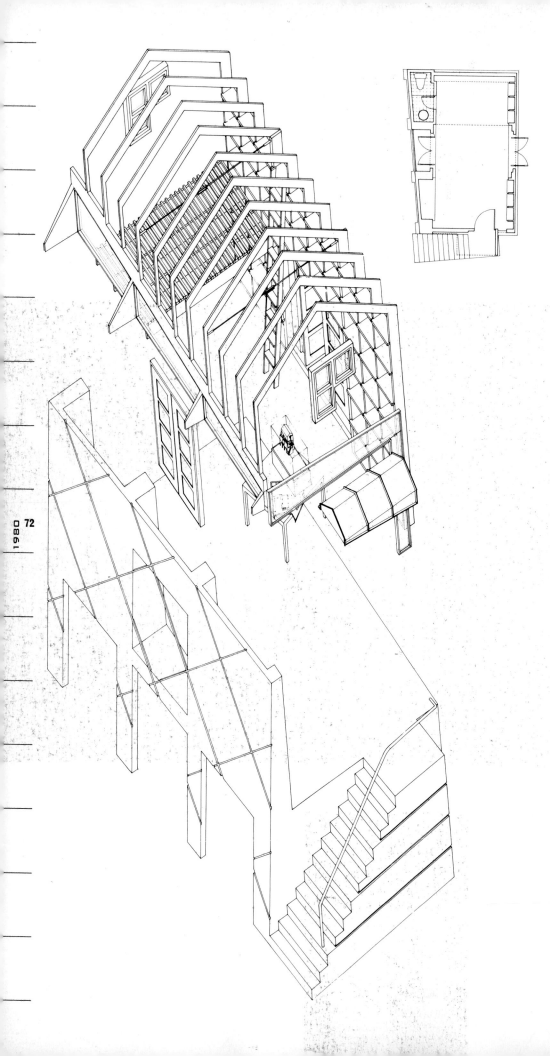

1980

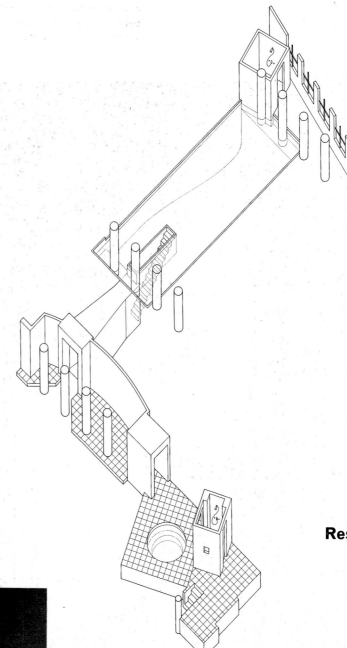

**Cohen
Residence**

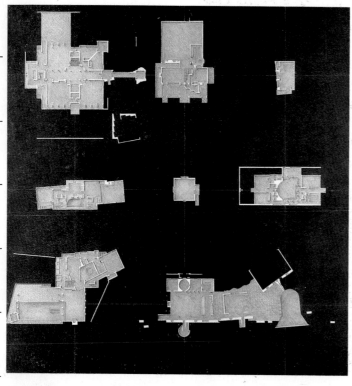

A two bedroom house for a middle-aged couple who are socially very active and who enjoy outdoor living and swimming had to be placed on two flat hillside pads at different heights and of different sizes.

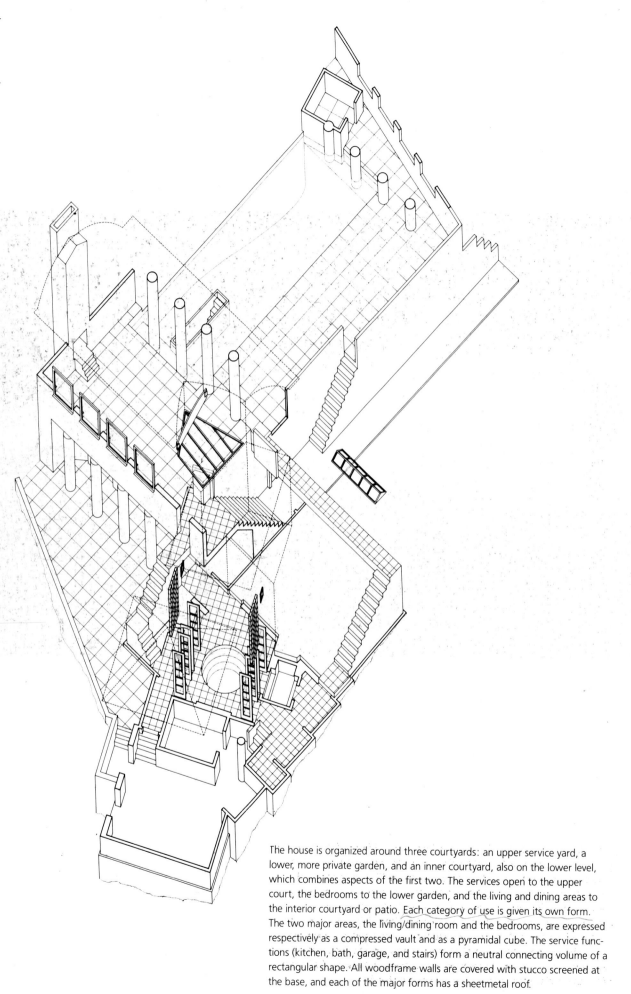

The house is organized around three courtyards: an upper service yard, a lower, more private garden, and an inner courtyard, also on the lower level, which combines aspects of the first two. The services open to the upper court, the bedrooms to the lower garden, and the living and dining areas to the interior courtyard or patio. Each category of use is given its own form. The two major areas, the living/dining room and the bedrooms, are expressed respectively as a compressed vault and as a pyramidal cube. The service functions (kitchen, bath, garage, and stairs) form a neutral connecting volume of a rectangular shape. All woodframe walls are covered with stucco screened at the base, and each of the major forms has a sheetmetal roof.

The autonomy of each part is reinforced by the inward focus of the rooms, by pushing all of the circulation to the exterior, and by the association of each programmatic element with its own outdoor space. The importance of the sequence of movement along the edges of the indoor and outdoor spaces is heightened by the symbolic development of the bathroom as *Bath*, the patio as *Court Pool* and the garden as *Lower Garden*. The building emulates indigenous Southwestern architecture by using thermal mass and by closing openings to the sun, except to the east, where morning sunlight filters into the living and kitchen spaces. On the west, which opens to the view, the impact of the sun is minimized by servo-operated exterior blinds.

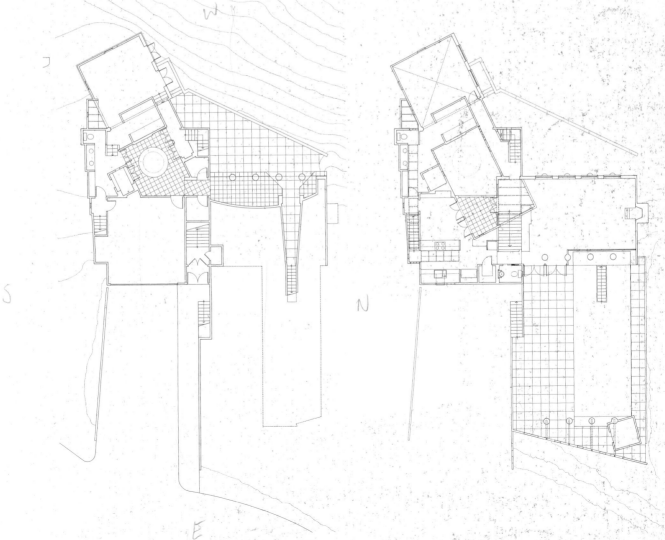

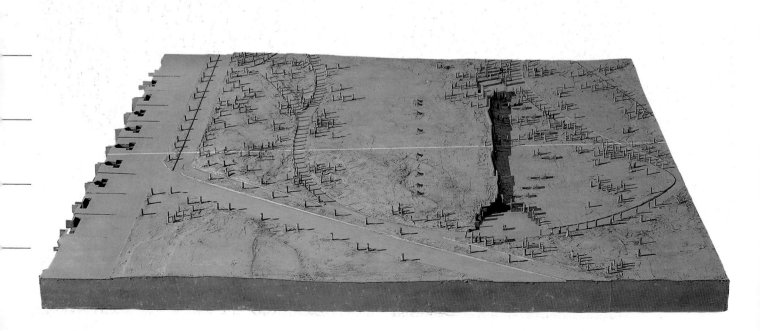

We wanted this project to confront one with the reality of death: one should not be able to sit and have lunch comfortably with the memory of the Vietnam War. Moreover, we realized that we could not build an object, since the site was not on the axes of the major monuments on the Washington Mall.

In order to design the project, we analyzed the statistics of the War, and realized that the death tolls from each year formed a bell curve: the amount of Americans killed rose gradually, then diminished. This condition was unlike that of most wars, where the death toll drops off suddenly at the end. Given this data and the site, we decided to make the monument a path that would lead one gradually down into the ground and then gradually back out.

The top of the walls separate the two halves of the site, making one aware of division, and also contain skylights. On descending the path from either end, one encounters niches or rooms that get progressively larger to contain the memory of the greater number of dead in each successive year. That memory is etched onto stone tablets that are disengaged from the wall to become the pillars that support the building, figuratively and metaphorically. In each room, a staircase rising to the light offers escape and release—but this release is frustrated by a grille separating one from this path. On the winter solistice, a shaft of sunlight will penetrate down through these skylights into each chamber, thus marking time and making one aware of winter, the death of nature.

Eventually, one rises out of the deepest and largest room in order to reach the landscape beyond this anti-monument.

Vietnam War Memorial

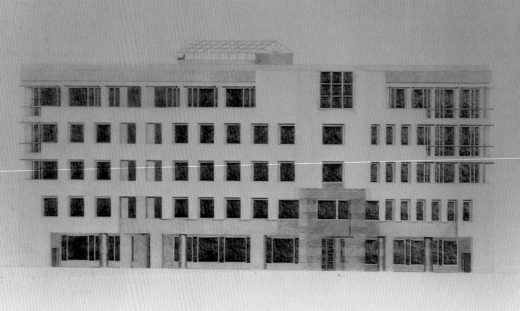

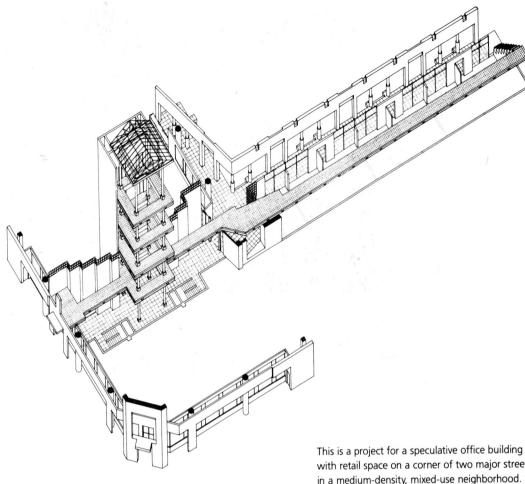

Western-Melrose
Office Building

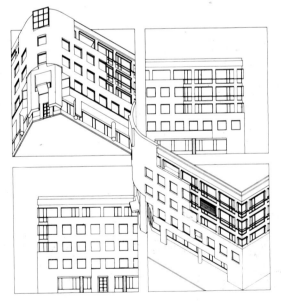

This is a project for a speculative office building with retail space on a corner of two major streets in a medium-density, mixed-use neighborhood. Two- and three-story "strip buildings" form the edges of housing blocks of single- and multi-family dwellings. The site is made up of two lots, which are offset from each other.

The main five-story building is on the front lot at the corner of the site. A two-story element extends to the second, back lot. This extension provides additional square footage while masking the rear façades of adjacent retail stores. Its articulation is scaled to the residential context.

Commercial spaces face the major streets and are entered from the front. The central lobby contains a full-height glazed atrium that serves a place-making function for the building. A loggia at the bottom of the rear extension leads to a two-story lobby.

This project explores the typology of walls in order to address both conceptual and practical issues. The wall, hung from a conventional steel rigid-frame structure, is used to produce a substantial corner for a building on a prominent site. It is made of glass window wall and cement asbestos panels in three colors, with stone used at the base, corner and columns. The wall changes its character and articulation to refer the building to its context, merging the two types which make up that context. Finally, the layered surface of the wall is used for sun control through the addition of retractable blinds.

Lawrence House

This house is a few hundred feet from the Pacific Ocean in a community characterized by a mix of single family homes and apartment complexes. The presence of the latter reflects a density which has been steadily increasing over the last twenty years.

The house responds to this urban situation by combining each of the two types of the context: a memory of the house originally on the site is placed within an apartment building-scaled block. The "house" accommodates a symmetrical entrance and basic functions such as stairs and bathrooms. It is the conceptual and spatial center of the building. The block, which is a metal-clad rectangular volume, slices diagonally through the site and is gridded to provide a datum against which the changing levels of floors can be read.

The major living spaces are located on the fourth floor to take advantage of ocean views over the roofs of neighboring houses, and the house is organized from the top down. The entry is located on an axis perpendicular to the long direction of the site, thus opening up the deepest interior of the building for the main organizing volume and for vertical circulation.

Windows are positioned to control views, privacy and light. Views are directed west, towards the ocean, and into the private gardens on the first and third floors. A single operable window in the kitchen on the south side of the building and a composition of three windows on the north side provide indirect light for the central space and reinforce the short axis.

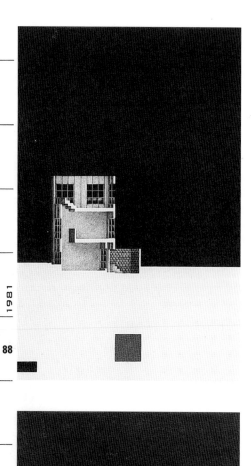

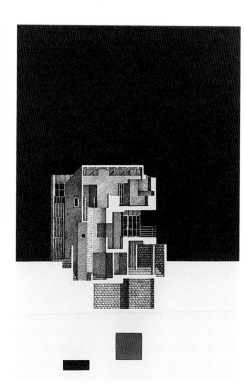

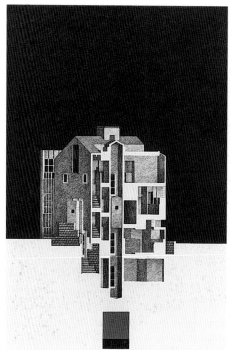

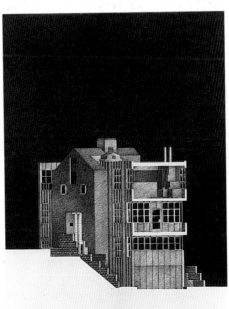
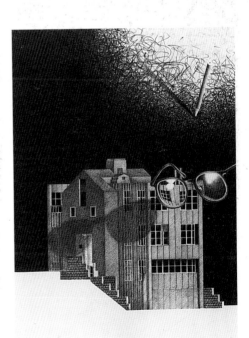

On the outside, the expression of the two pieces is purposefully banal, thus camouflaging the spatially diverse, unpredictable and idiosyncratic nature of the interior. The shingle siding, galvanized metal roof, wood windows and glass block of the house piece are contrasted with the metal windows and siding of the block.

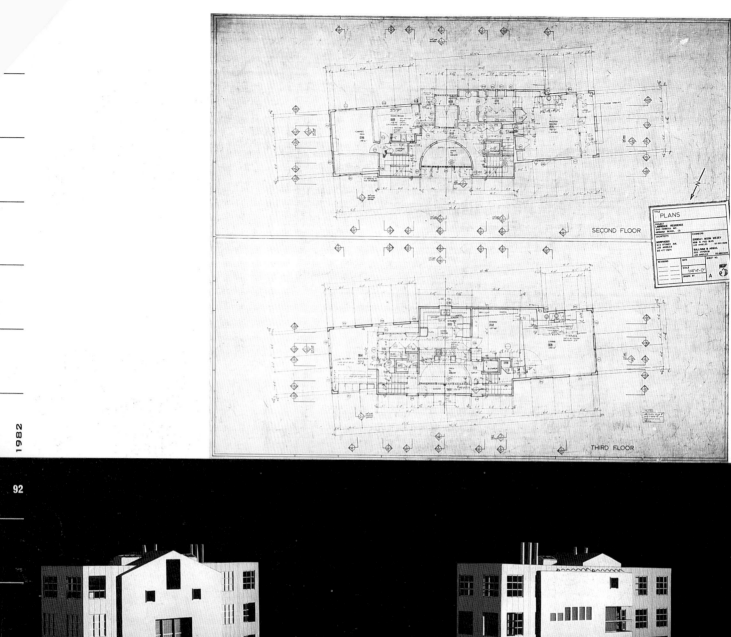

SECOND FLOOR

THIRD FLOOR

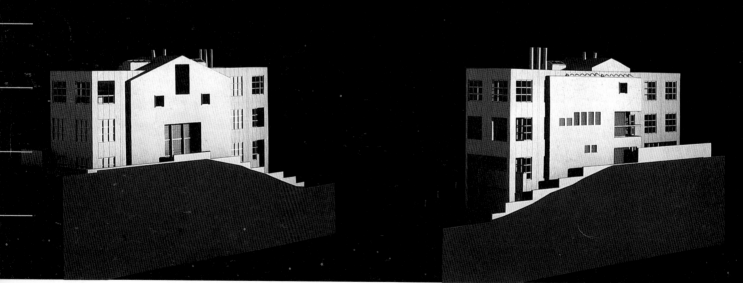

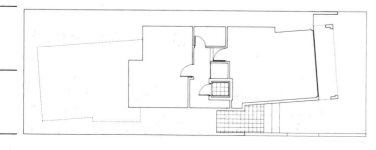
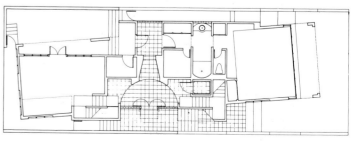

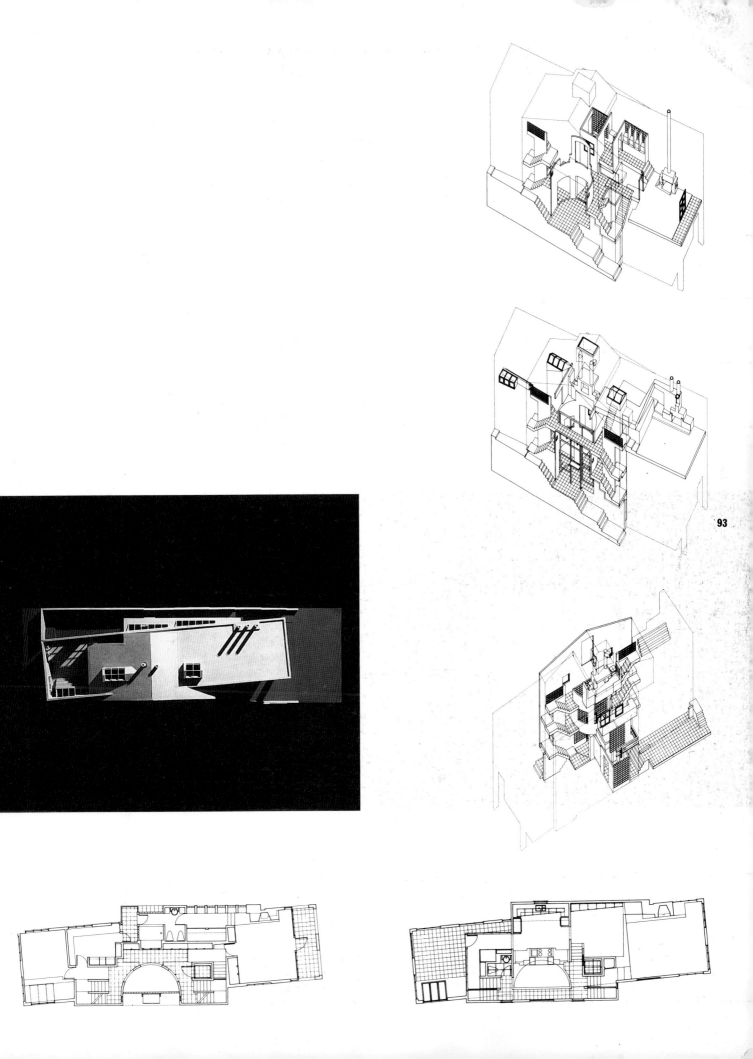

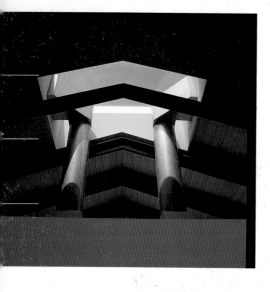

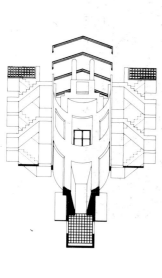

The city of Hermosa Beach owned two adjacent parcels of land at the end of a pier. The sites, located between the ocean front walk and the main commercial street of the city, were being used as parking lots, and the city asked for a proposal for alternative uses.

Our plan intensified the central business district while clarifying and ordering existing, but disparate elements through the development of a continuity of spatial arrangements. The site was composed as a triangle focusing on the pier. The south site was organized around a plaza. Retail stores lined the street, while a civic amphitheater, a gallery and a formal entrance space occupied the plaza. The building height and design was meant to respond to a context of bungalows at the south.

The north site was developed into a series of small court spaces surrounded by stores and offices and terminating in a much smaller public plaza. The linear slabs which organize this complex focused the site on the pier and linked the ocean front walk to the main street. The massive nature of this extension of the downtown area was mediated by breaking down the slabs into articulated pieces to the north. These pieces were designed to reinforce the connection to the adjoining residential area. A linear path utilized an existing commercial arcade and connected the two sites at mid-block. The complex opened up the city back to the pier, answered to the city's desire for small scale development preserving views and heights, and maintained and further developed the existing grid of urban blocks inherent to much of the area.

Hermosa Beach Central Business District

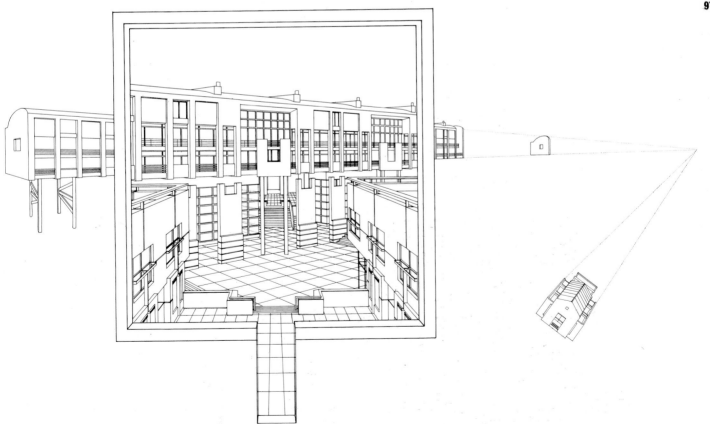

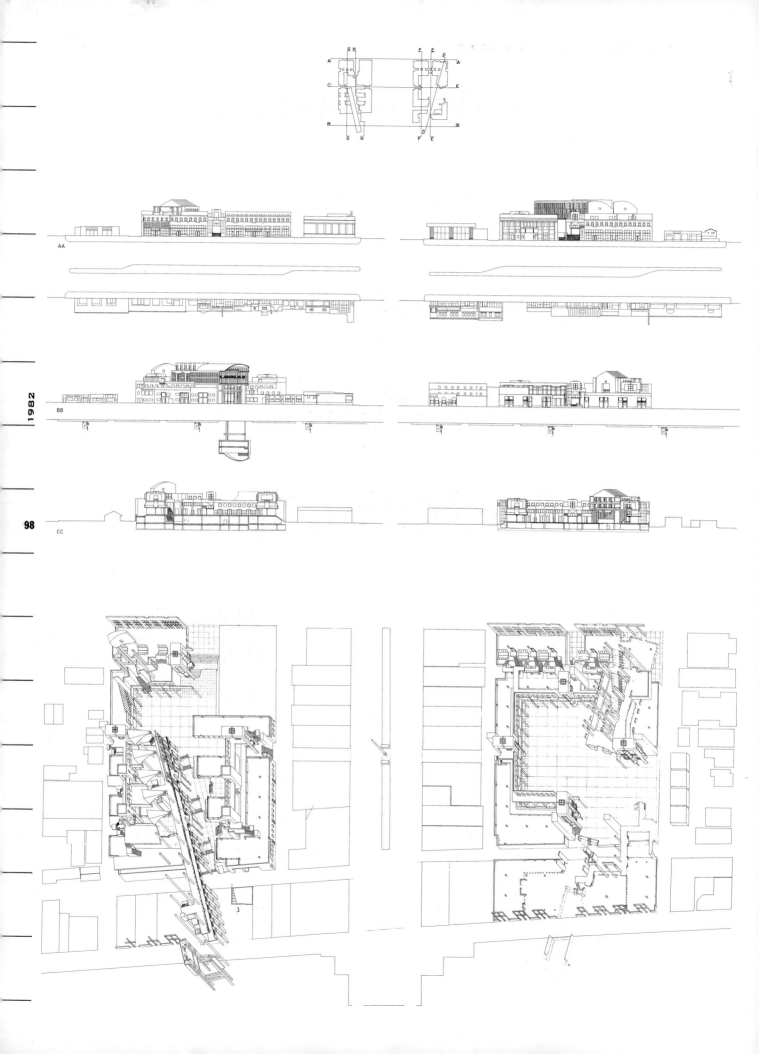

AA

BB

CC

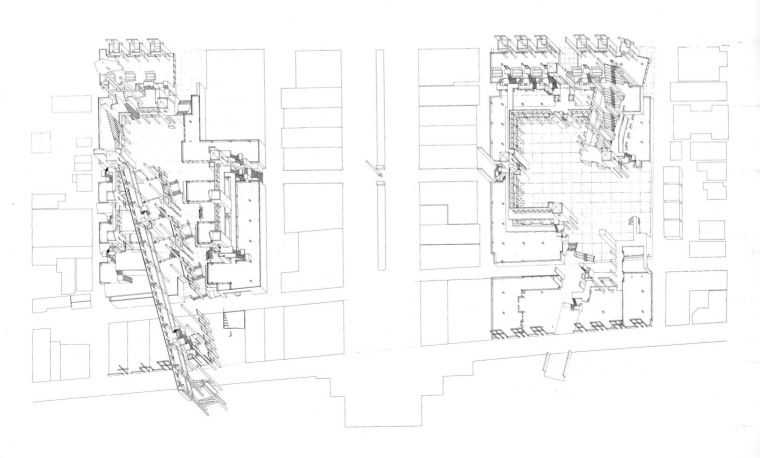

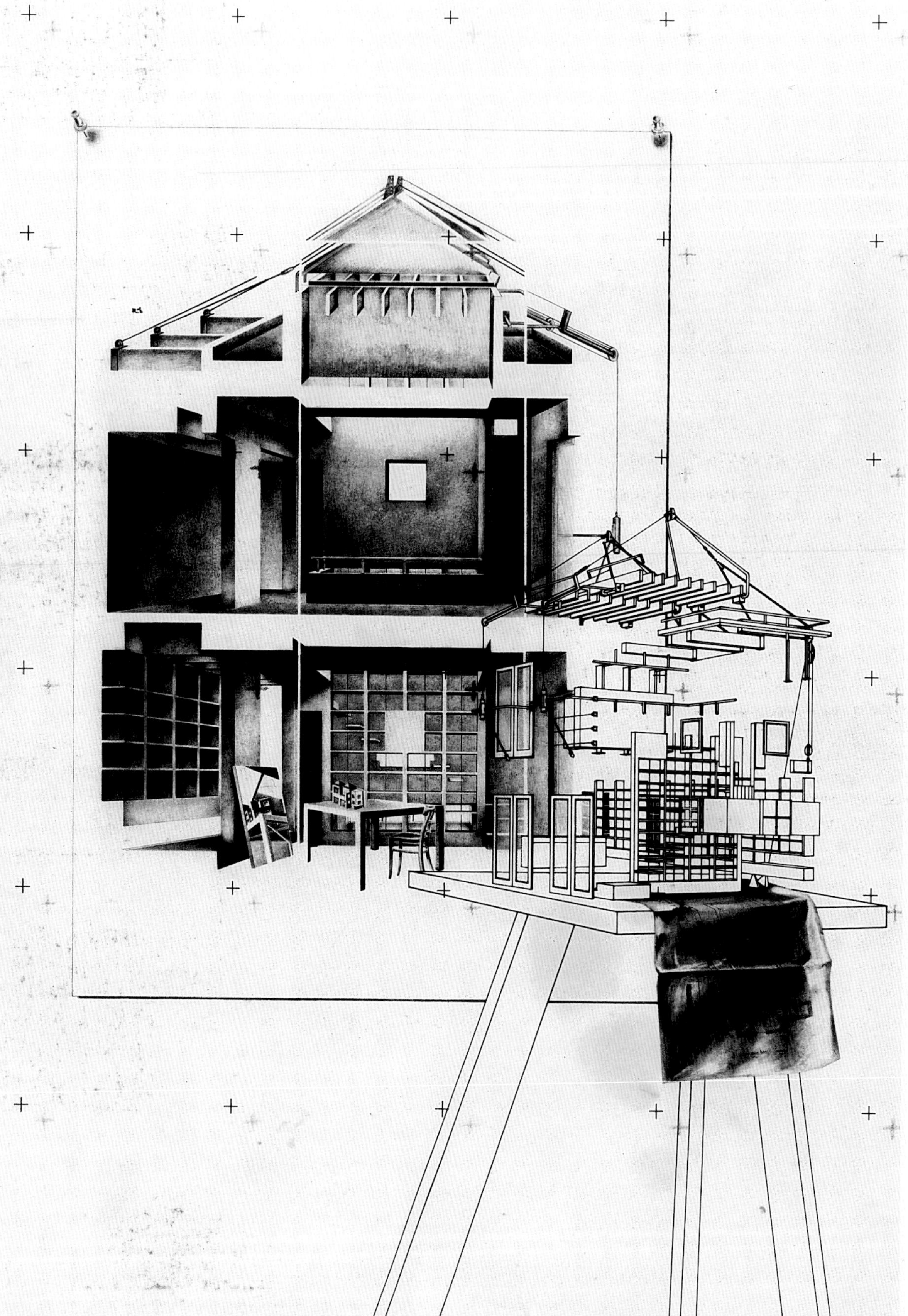

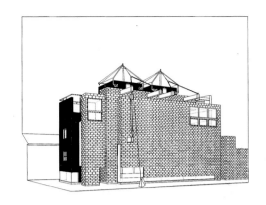

Venice III

A library, work area, bedroom, bathroom, and deck have been added to the rear of a 40 by 80 foot lot in a community characterized by small bungalow-type houses. The building consists of three articulated parts. The largest element is a rectilinear volume containing the work area on the ground level and a bedroom above. The second piece, which runs along the northern edge of the first, is a long, thin space, containing a dressing room on top of a library. The third element has three components. These parts transform themselves from mere skylights to a skylight over a two-story volume to a small, semi-attached rear building that includes a future kitchen, a bathroom and a deck.

The addition was conceived of as a prototype for a scaled-down urban house for a small family on a restricted urban lot. The character and the physical organization of the new structure allow it to operate as an extension of the existing house, as a separate area to be used for members of an extended family, and a separate dwelling that could be rented or sold. The addition is made of concrete slab, wood frame, asphalt shingle walls and metal wall panels.

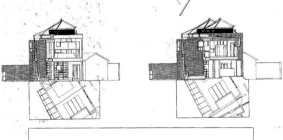

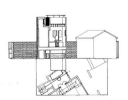

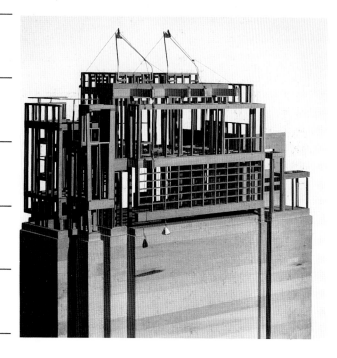

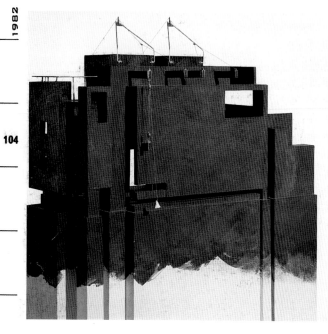

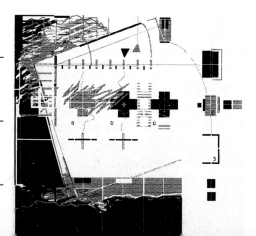

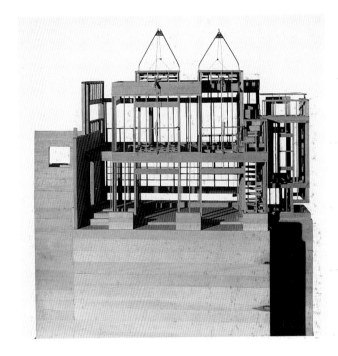

1982

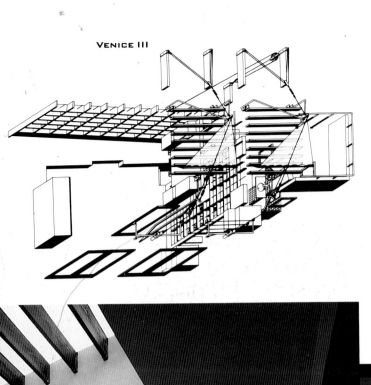

VENICE III

111

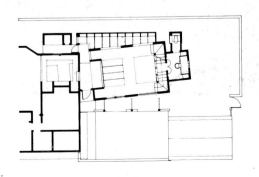

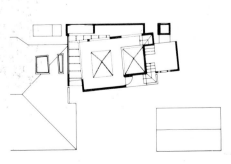

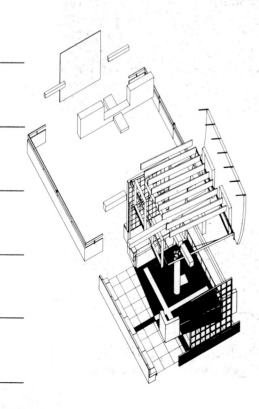

This restaurant is a new piece of construction utilizing a historic building on a small street of rich architectural heritage in Venice. The building is part of the original collonaded texture of downtown Venice. Central to the renovation is a new column, aligned with the cast-iron column of the front façade, which literally helps to support the old building: the etched metal post, placed in the middle of a cubical bar area, supports an earthquake tension ring. The existing slender column is contrasted with a short, thick and hollow metal construction with a bolted capital supporting only horizontal loads. The "main room" is straightforward and simple, seating sixty people in a rectangle left-over between the front and the back. The project addresses issues of loss of center, destabilization, and the breaking and making of architecture. It is meant to be perceived as a permanent building in a city that worships the ephemeral.

72 Market Street Restaurant

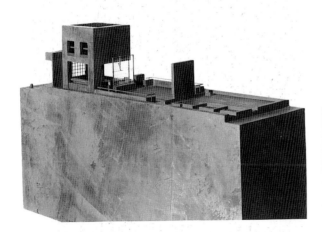

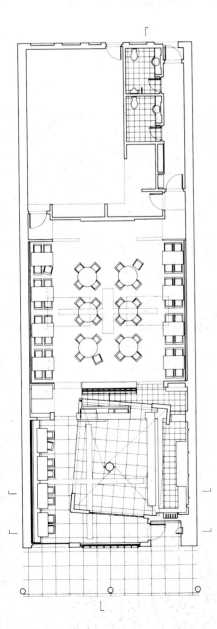

Our work at the Hennessy and Ingalls bookstore in Santa Monica attempts to reinterpret an existing quasi-art deco building into something more abstract. A new assembly of fragments of columns, pieces of storefronts and metal gridworks simultaneously reinforces and subverts the original. The original symmetry of the façade has been made incomplete and has been violated. A steel beam emphasizes balance in juxtaposition to the existing slab-like turret

Hennessy and Ingalls

and also supports an entrance canopy. The façade evidences an interest in weight and mass described by the materiality of the built project and by the energy implicit within the process of its making.

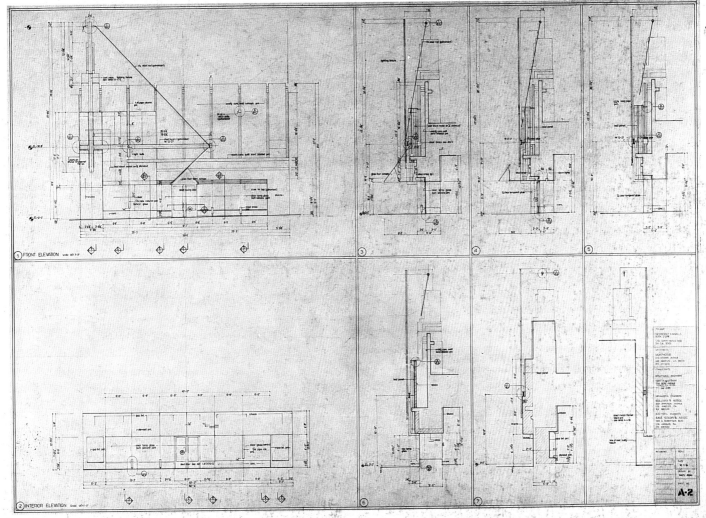

A partial gridwork was added to the façade of a building on Melrose Avenue in Los Angeles as an inexpensive way of making and marking an addition. The façade was meant to appear as if it predated the existing building. By using minimal means, it creates a series of shifts in foreground/background meaning. The interior of the restaurant seats forty-five in two sections, with a bar and kitchen toward the rear.

Entry to the first part of this two-phase conversion covering two stores is through a door which has been suppressed and made invisible from the facade. All one sees from the street is a series of planes and a beam penetrating the outside wall from the inside.

Angeli Restaurant

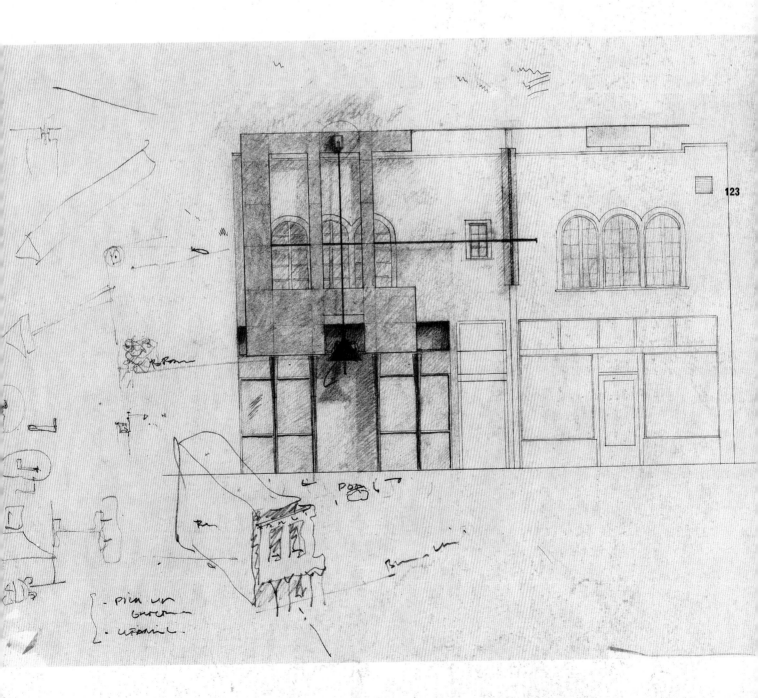

123

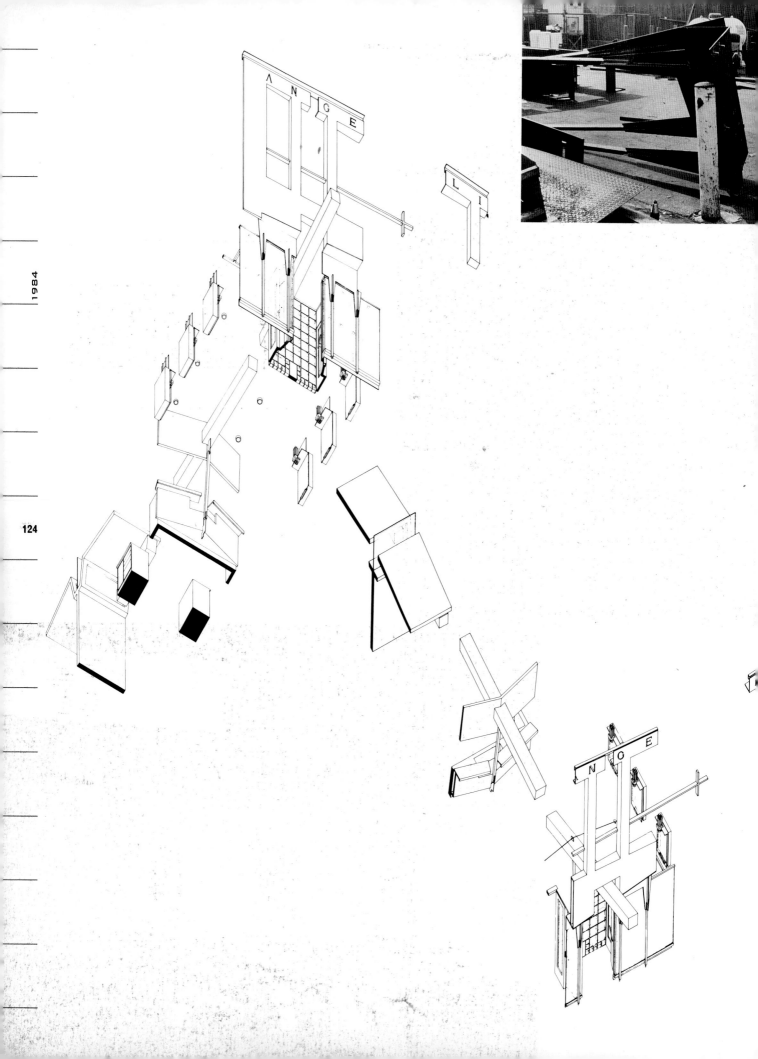

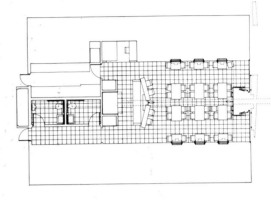

A Table of Two

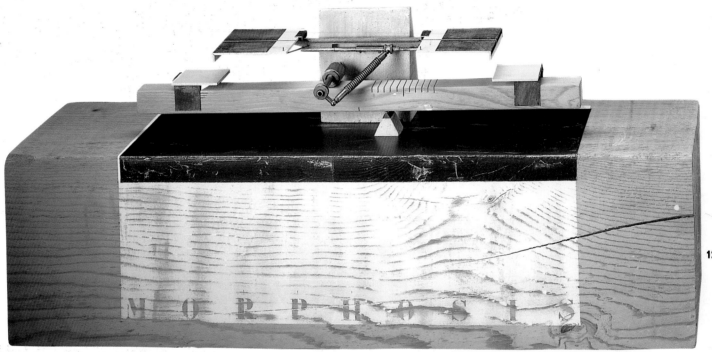

Imagine a table that can only be used by two people who agree to sit down at the same time and to remain seated until they agree to get up. The table forces one to make choices that involve consent, dependency and risk. The table operates on the principle of a fulcrum. When the weight of two people is correctly distributed, the beam and the two table tops which make up this four by twelve foot object remain horizontal; otherwise the beam's position is diagonal and the table tops rotate upwards. The fulcrum length of the beam can be adjusted by sliding it horizontally between two rollers at top and bottom. These rollers are part of a steel assembly which transfers the upward thrust of the beam diagonally through a springed shock absorber. The assembly is attached at three points to a concrete mass which keeps the entire object in a fixed position. Imagine an object, perhaps a table, that is expressed in terms of how it is made and is made in a way that reveals how it operates.

128

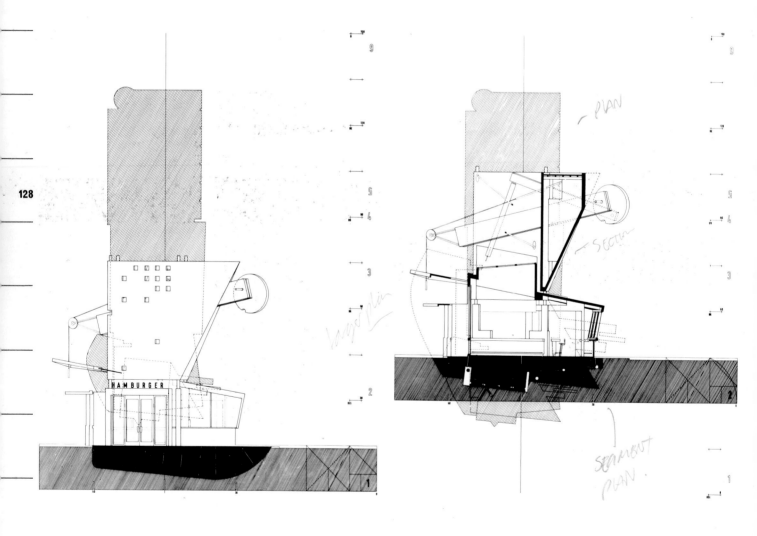

HAMBURGER

Hamburger Stand

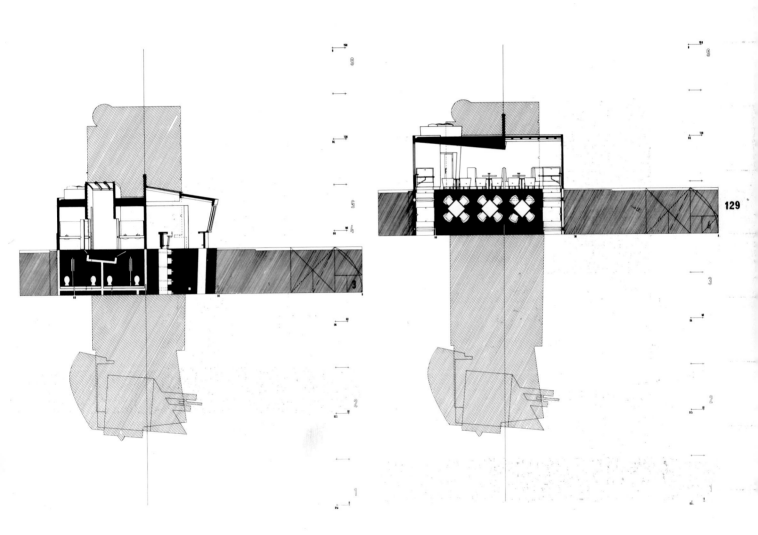

129

This project, located on a typical corner site of a typical commercial building strip, develops the *stand* as a building type familiar to the Los Angeles area. 2,500 square feet of space are required for both walk-in and auto take-out food service, as well as for seating 142 people. The various programmatic requirements are standard to the Amercian hamburger ethic.

The stand aspires simultaneously to the energy, the movement, and the making aspects of the machine, and to its decay and death—a machine as both creator and destroyer. The project rejects the contention of architecture as optimization of advanced technology. It is androgynous. It is not patriotic. It has no interest in "good taste."

1984

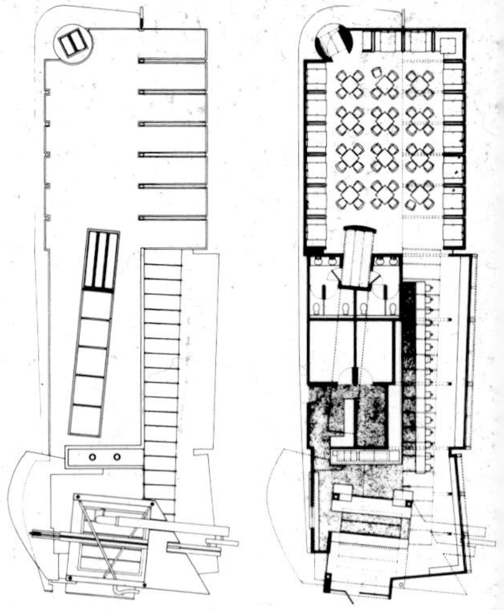

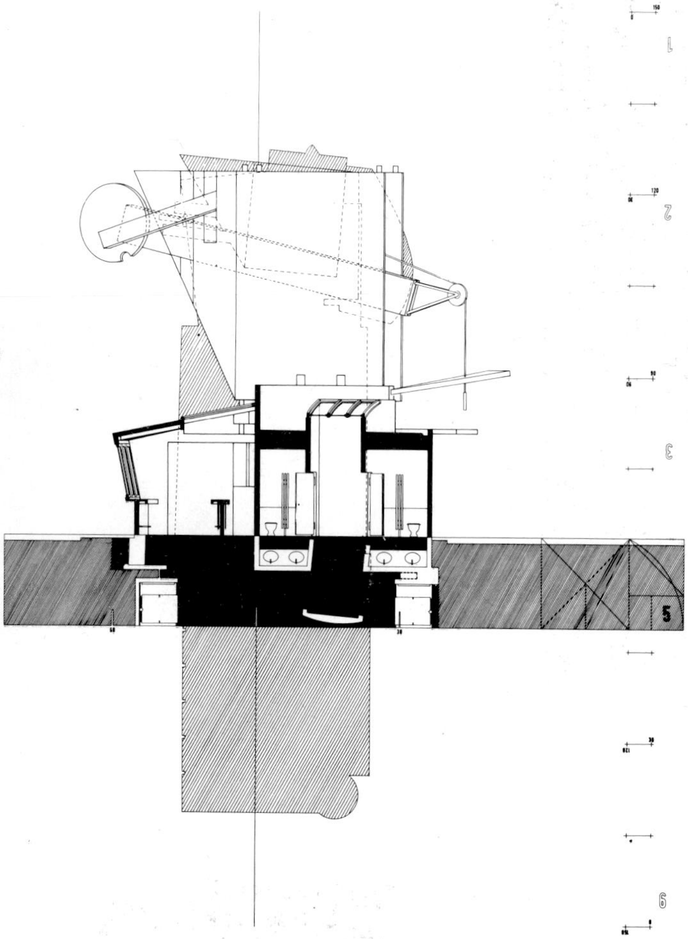

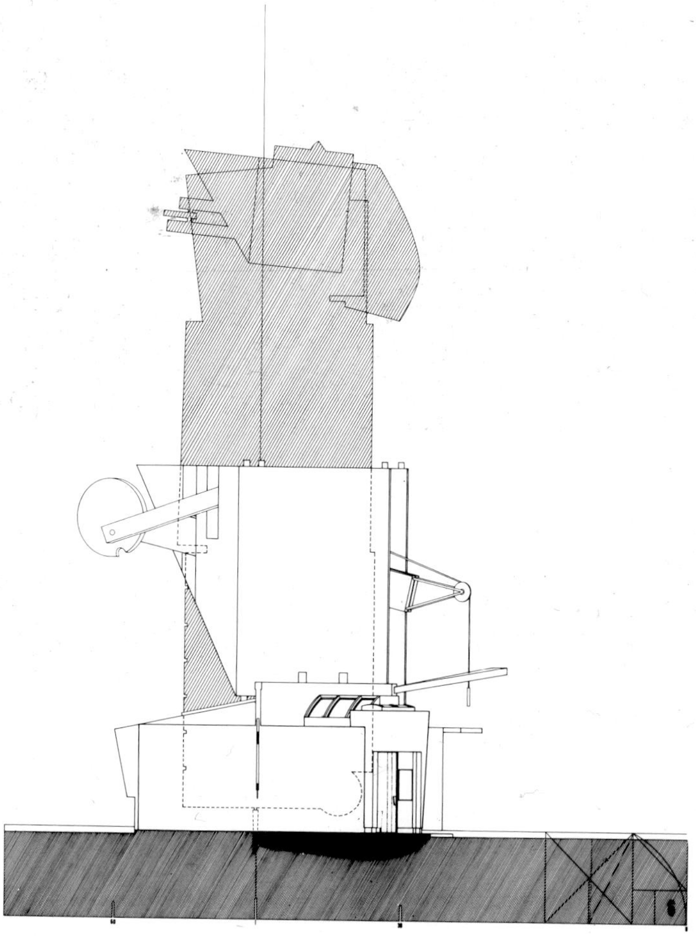

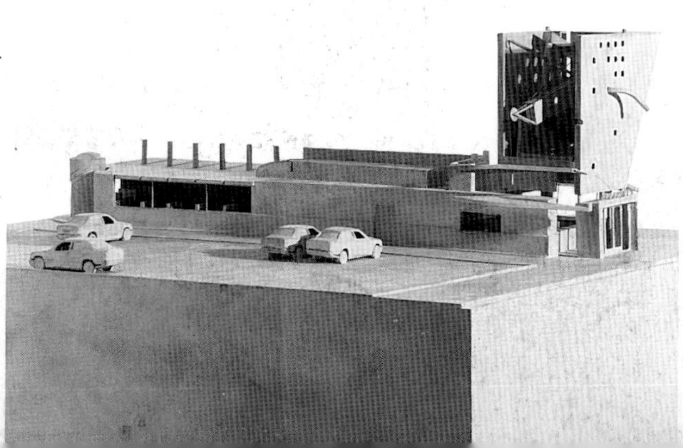

Kate Mantilini Restaurant

Our client wanted "a roadside steakhouse for the future, with a clock," a hybrid cafe/restaurant/diner to be placed in a nineteen-fifties bank building on Wilshire Boulevard in Beverly Hills. Rather than merely renovating the interior, we created an active *poche* wall engulfing the old frame, and designed on a four-person booth increment. An oculus was cut into the ceiling, and into that oculus a notionally kinetic orrery was placed. This metal construction describes the plan of the building on the floor. A curving wall over the long bar and kitchen area depicts—at the request of the client —the pre-War fight promoter for whom the restaurant was named.

The space in which this takes place is aggressive, obsessive, and active, though it is tempered by a certain coolness and a business-like politeness. It is a simple open hall, vaguely exterior in character, reflecting its public intention. The massiveness of the booth-wall gives the whole structure a permanence, while the grid of the interior is carried to the outside, so that the skin has a cactus-like appearance, vacillating between surface and volume. This project requires a "reading" in terms other than those of sight alone.

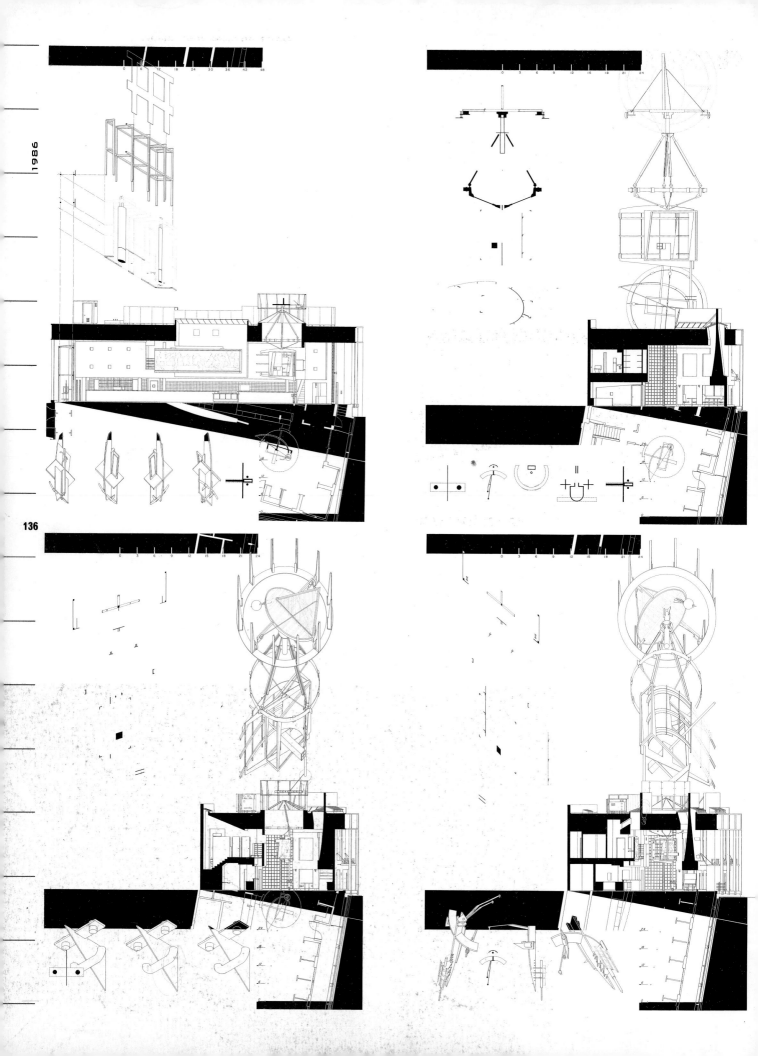

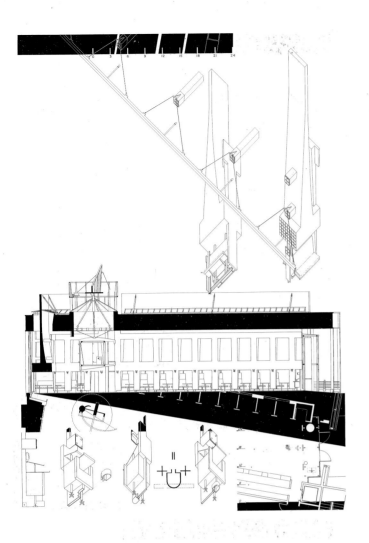

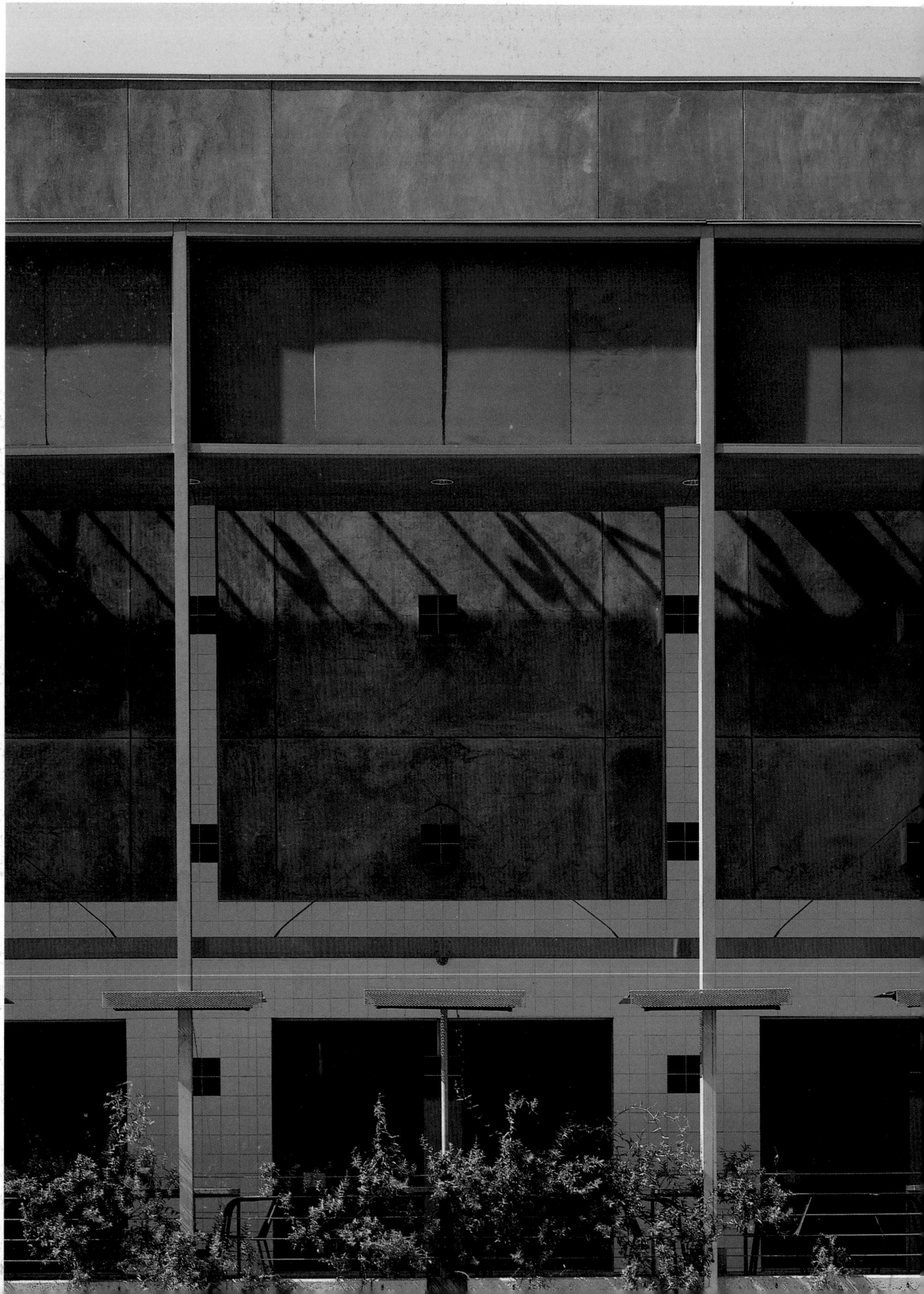

139

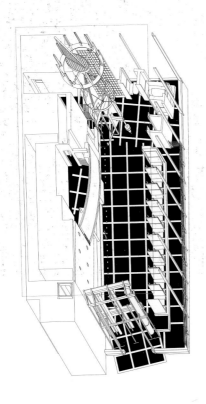

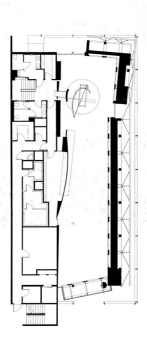

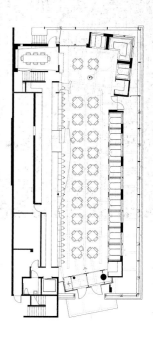

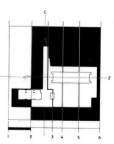

144

The Comprehensive Cancer Center is an out-patient facility for the treatment of cancer, which combines diagnosis, treatment and counseling in one setting. It is part of the Cedars-Sinai Medical Center in Los Angeles, located on and under a parking lot and helipad at the northeast corner of this large hospital complex. Well over half the space is below grade. The new Center had to maintain a direct connection to an existing subterranean radiation therapy department located within the Medical Center. The desire to minimize patient movement and to give the Center its own identity—since the patients maintain relatively normal lifestyles during the course of their treatment—led to the placement of the treatment floor at the lowest level, while the main entry to the facility is at ground level.

We utilized a clear functional strategy to make sense out of this difficult site and the complex components of the program. The whole Center was organized around two large spaces, an atrium/treatment area and a waiting room, both of which rise up from the lowest level to street grade. The waiting area is adjacent to the existing building, and the atrium "centers" the more eastern section of the facility. A main axis runs perpendicular to these two areas and connects them to the main reception functions at grade level. A laboratory and a pharmacy face the waiting area, while minor procedure rooms and nurse stations gird the atrium/treatment area. A series of corridors connects these two groups of activities to clinical areas, doctor's offices, and other ancillary functions.

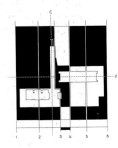

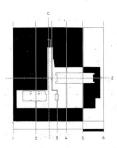

This organizational strategy is realized in an architecture emphasizing the vertical nature of the Center. This architecture is meant to enhance one's comprehension of location and choice of movement within this facility by focusing on the entry of light into this dark place and by utilizing overt references to construction. The waiting area and the atrium were conceived of as quasi-exterior spaces, and create a datum out of the relationship of a new ground plane and the sky. A framework of geometries, similar and diverse in character, establishes the various departments as autonomous pieces. The patient, visitor and worker orients him- or herself though the perception and understanding of these discrete units and their particular architectural properties. Service and ancillary spaces were left as "generic," in order to reinforce this comprehension.

The architecture is made out of the manipulation of and emphasis on surfaces, not through the making of objects. The constructional articulation of surfaces allows the patient to understand the architecture as rooted in a physical reality. Yet this architecture is also meant to occupy the mind and affect the spirit, thus acting as a foil to the patient's current circumstances by removing him or her from self-concern. A "play-structure" in the waiting area is the one autonomous object in this dense Center, and it represents our objectives. It is a construction which engages children through the use of video, movable parts that can be operated by hand, and a small theater-like space. It entertains the mind with notions pertaining to the building's own construction and with fragments of the urban mechanisms. Rooted in fishtanks and rising up to a tree, it presents man-made constructs in relationship to the wholeness and simplicity of nature, while being permeated with the folly of a Dr. Seuss.

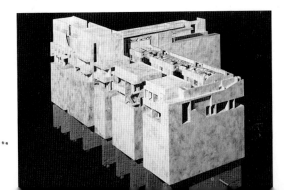

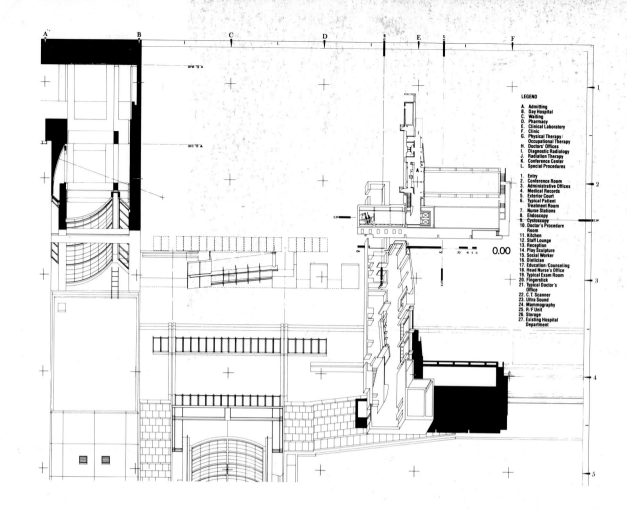

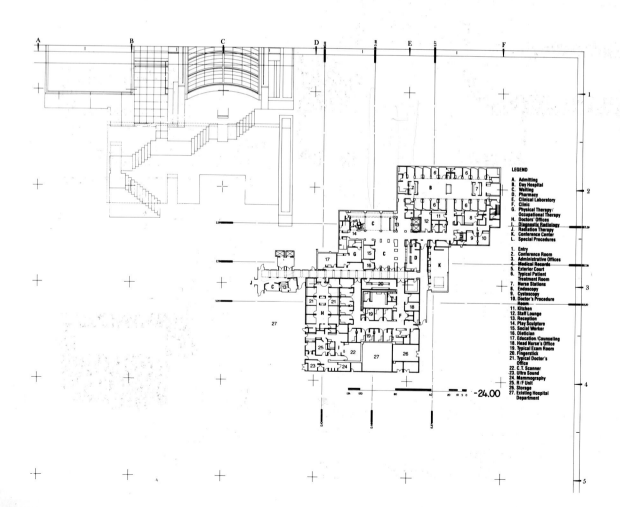

LEGEND

A. Admitting
B. Day Hospital
C. Waiting
D. Pharmacy
E. Clinical Laboratory
F. Clinic
G. Physical Therapy/
   Occupational Therapy
H. Doctors' Offices
I. Diagnostic Radiology
J. Radiation Therapy
K. Conference Center
L. Special Procedures

1. Entry
2. Conference Room
3. Administrative Offices
4. Medical Records
5. Exterior Court
6. Typical Patient
   Treatment Room
7. Nurse Stations
8. Endoscopy
9. Cystoscopy
10. Doctor's Procedure
    Room
11. Kitchen
12. Staff Lounge
13. Reception
14. Play Sculpture
15. Social Worker
16. Dietician
17. Education/Counseling
18. Head Nurse's Office
19. Typical Exam Room
20. Fingerstick
21. Typical Doctor's
    Office
22. C.T. Scanner
23. Ultra Sound
24. Mammography
25. R/F Unit
26. Storage
27. Existing Hospital
    Department

146

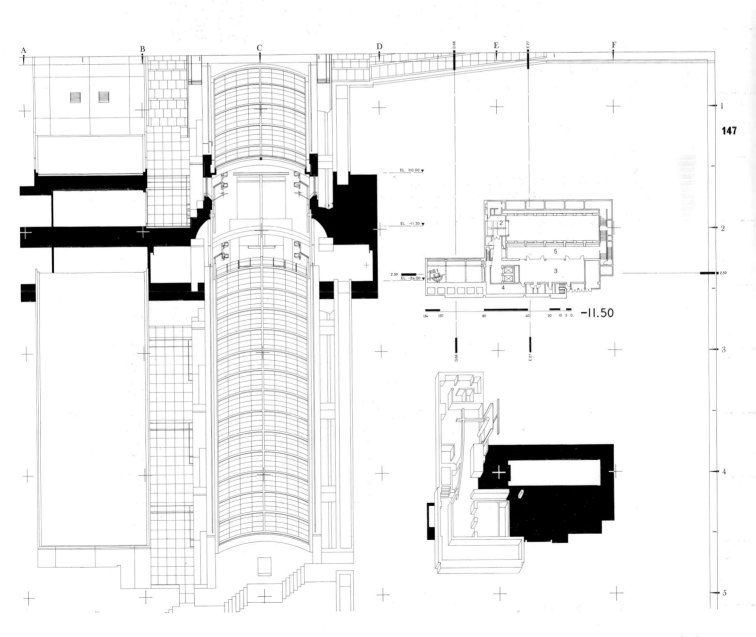

147

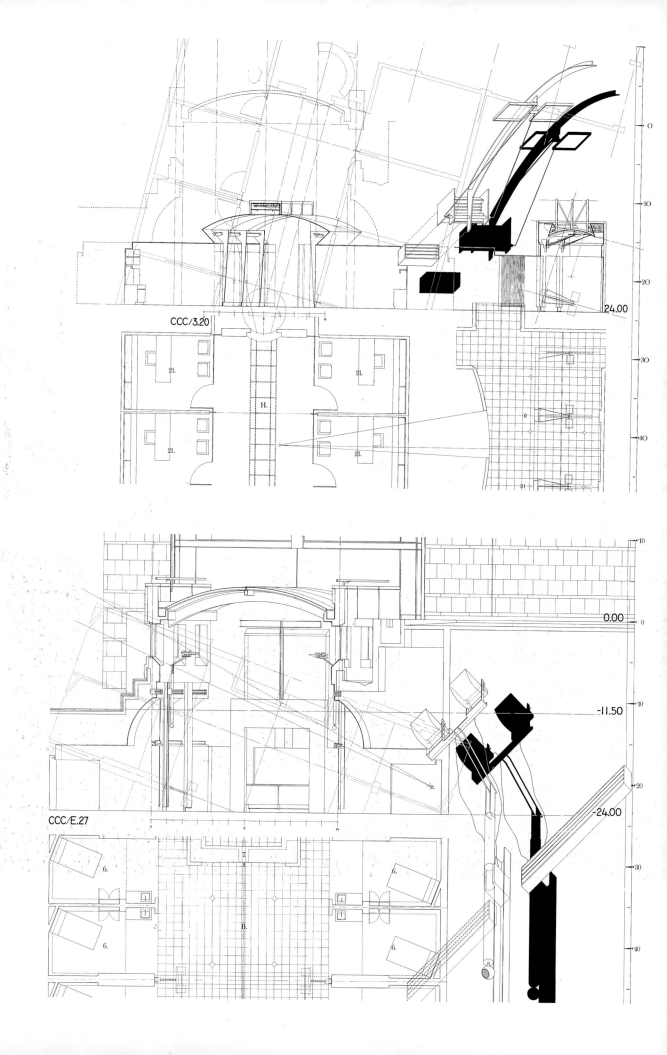

CCC/3.20

24.00

CCC/E.27

0.00

-11.50

-24.00

148

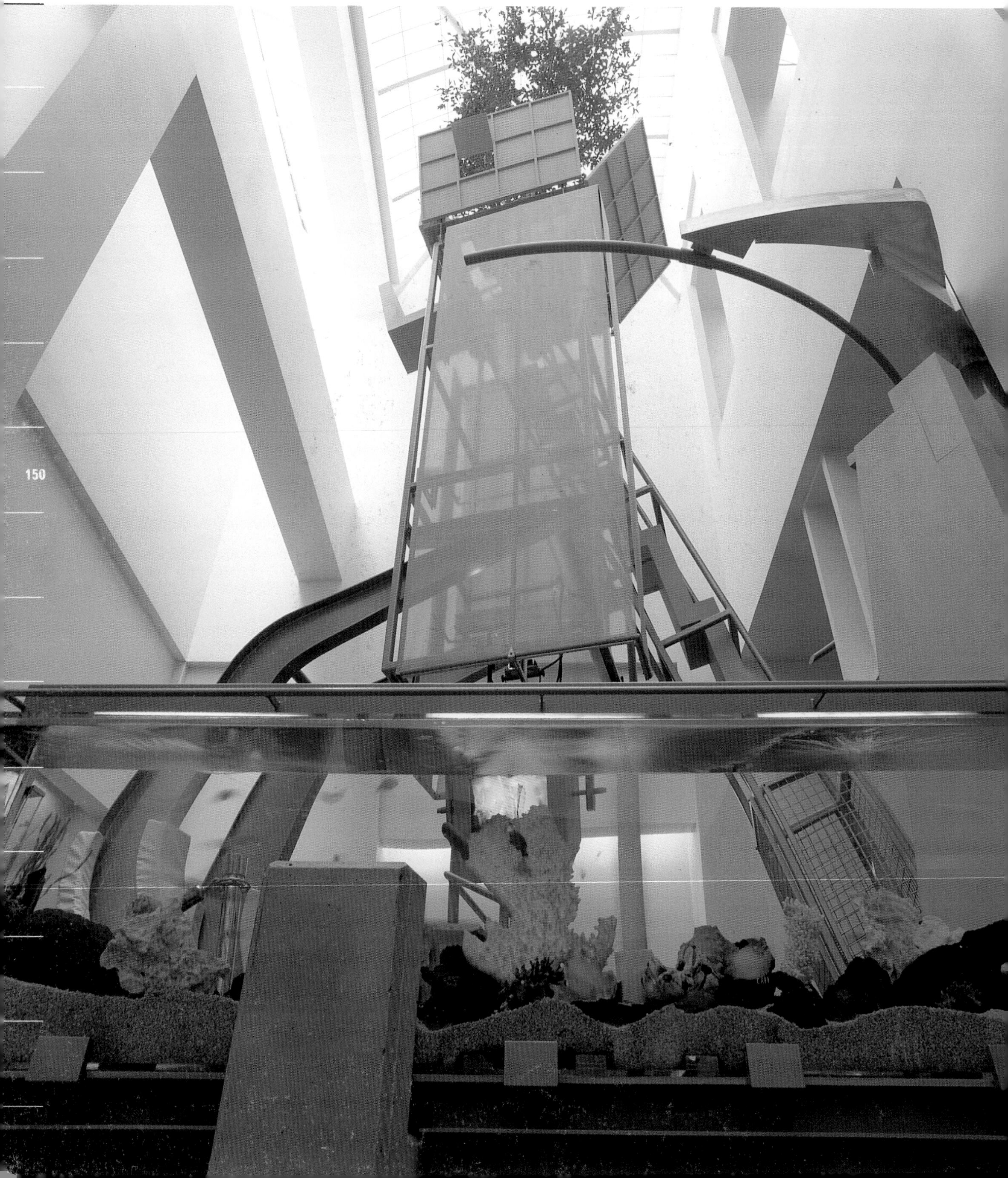

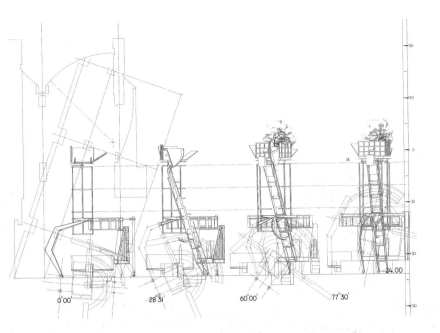

0°00' 28°31' 60°00' 77°30'

24.00

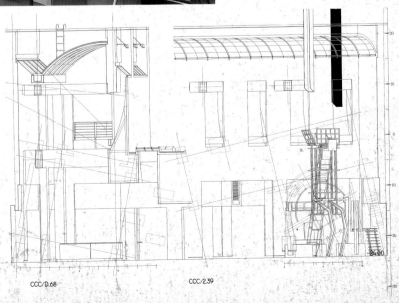

CCC/D.68   CCC/2.39

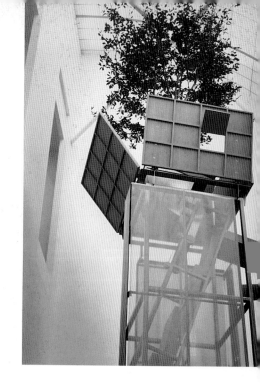

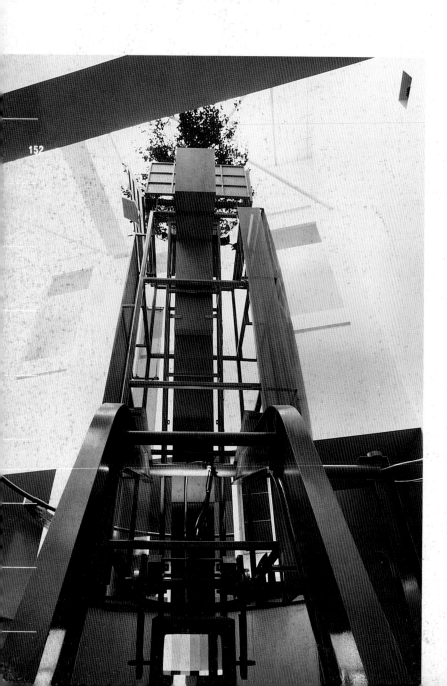

152

153

154

The creation of an interior space within an existing building for the display and sale of a continually changing collection of women's apparel provided an opportunity to explore the power of illumination, elevation, and obfuscation in the marketing process.

A *wrapper* or *liner,* made up of movable modular units having a perforated surface, was created to store mechandise while simultaneously providing space for private offices. A seasonal variation in color is perceived as fabrics emerge through the translucency of this screen wall, which reinforces existing spatial boundaries and functions as a backdrop for four free-standing objects. These objects (suggestive of machinery, the *process of production)* accomodate the reception, runway, conference room, and client waiting area. Beyond referring to the dynamic aspect of the *making process,* they also establish a dialogue with the permanent architecture of the building.

155

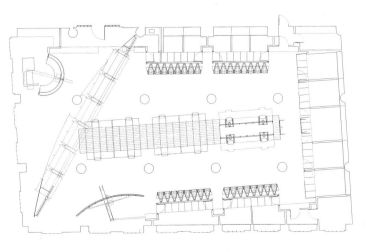

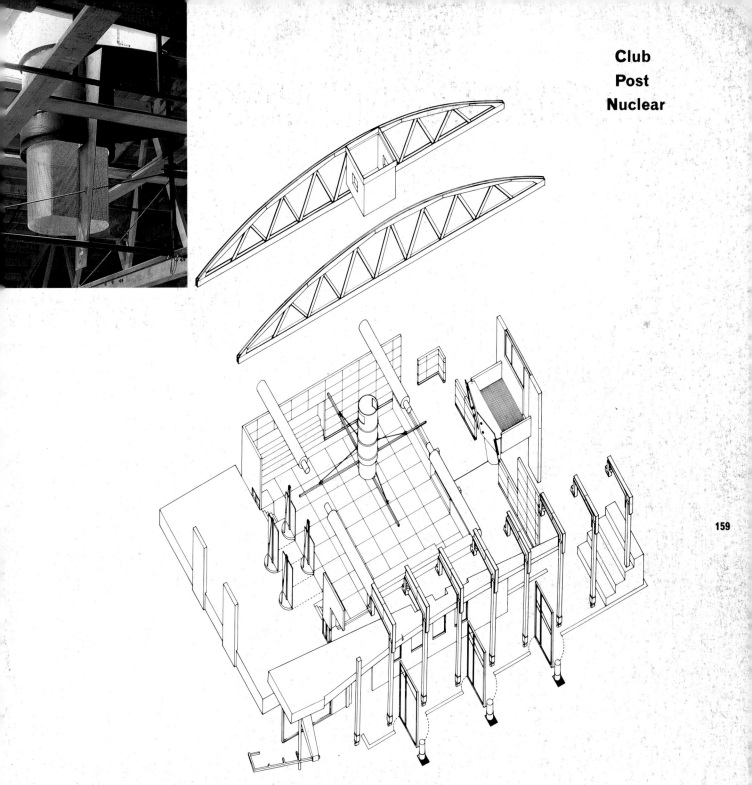

This nightclub/cafe is in an industrial building fronting a major highway a mile-and-a-half inland from the Pacific Ocean in Laguna Beach, California. Club Post Nuclear is made up of an espresso bar and sidewalk cafe, a dance center and a non-alcoholic nightclub for youths. A new concrete exterior wraps around the existing building in order to toughen its character, while the lobby spans both interior and exterior to reflect the public intention of the program.

The building is meant to reflect its clientele: it is aggressive, raw, exaggerated, and tempered by simplicity. The architecture is also meant to make people extremely conscious of their pose. Club Post Nuclear exhibits our continuing interest in an architecture composed of a series of independent, yet connected pieces, and in spaces housing simple functions which have been pushed, distorted or aggrandized.

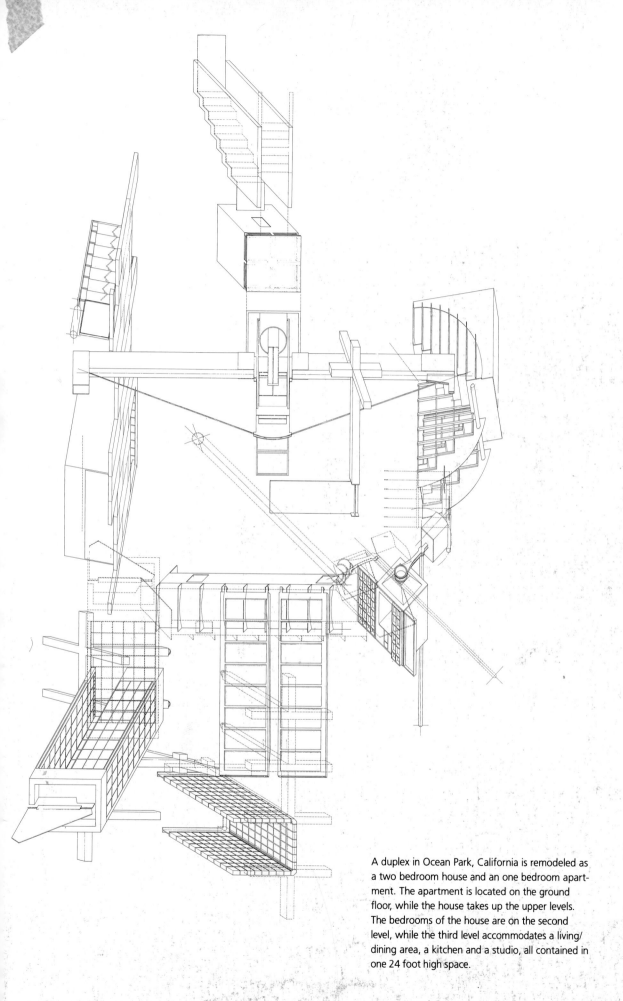

A duplex in Ocean Park, California is remodeled as a two bedroom house and an one bedroom apartment. The apartment is located on the ground floor, while the house takes up the upper levels. The bedrooms of the house are on the second level, while the third level accommodates a living/dining area, a kitchen and a studio, all contained in one 24 foot high space.

The main living space of the house is meant to re-create the loft in which the owner formerly lived. The architecture of the house is an attempt to address the surrounding, the conflicting demands for privacy and connection to society through a contemporary archaeology and the use of found objects. The foundation, perimeter walls and floors of the existing duplex are reused. The wood frame, lath, and cement composition board structure of the renovation will remain uncovered. Ten fabricated steel pieces, made up of found parts of machinery, have been inserted into the living space. These are functional objects; they are made into structure, stairs, showers, skylights and other utilitarian elements. Each piece performs several functions at the same time.

164

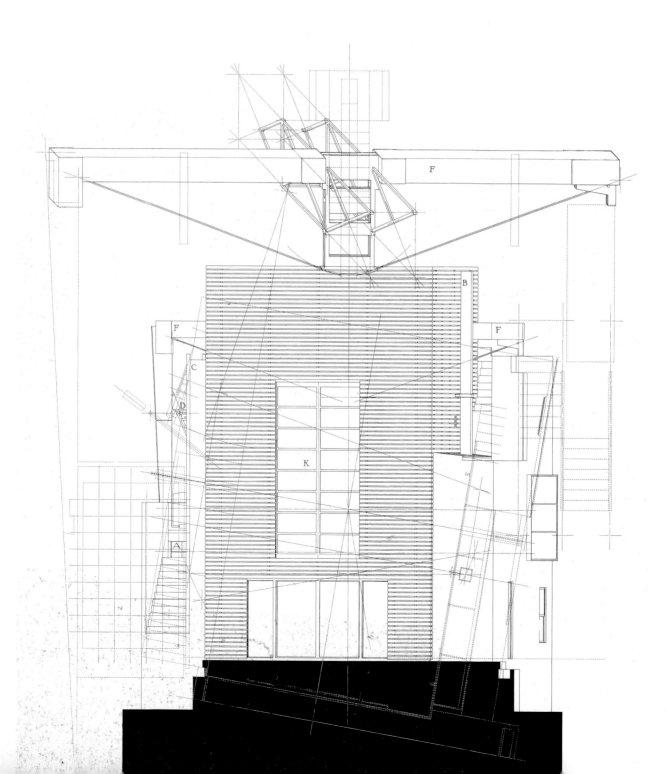

While the exterior of the house is contextual and traditional, and thus protects the private world of the interior with a facade of formality, the "dead tech" pieces on the inside import a technological world into the very heart of the house.

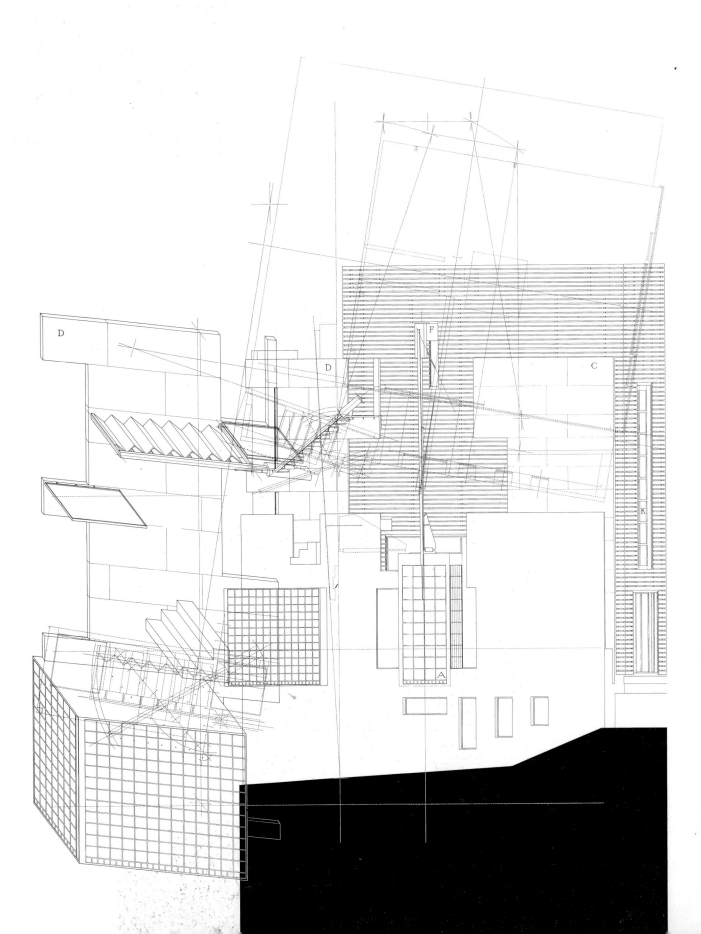

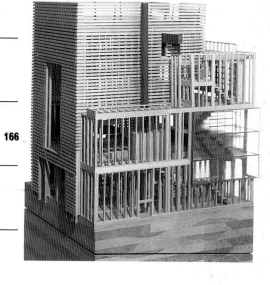

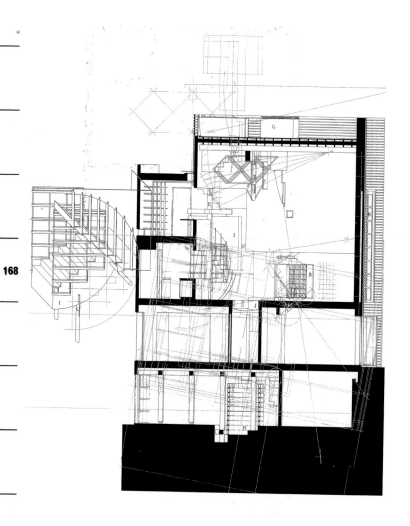

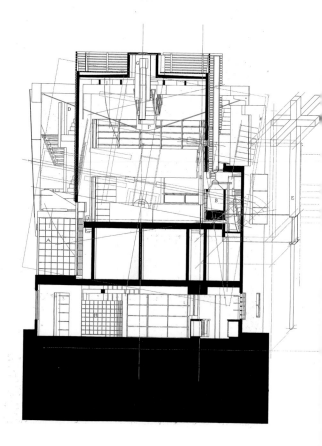

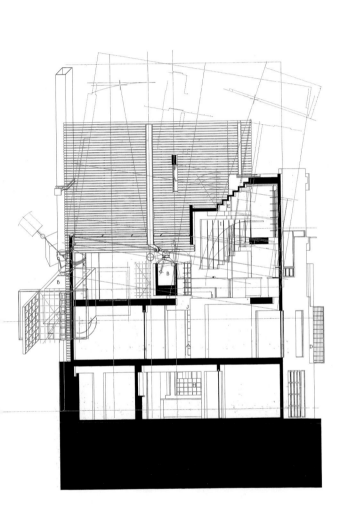

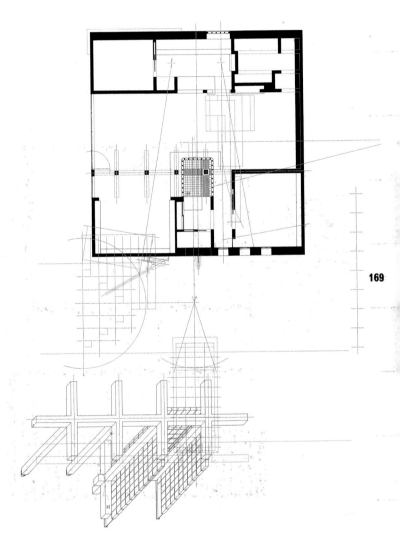

169

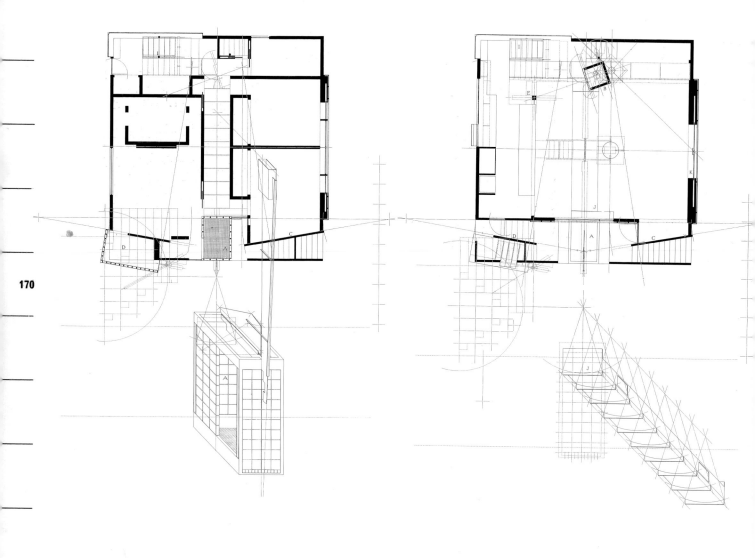

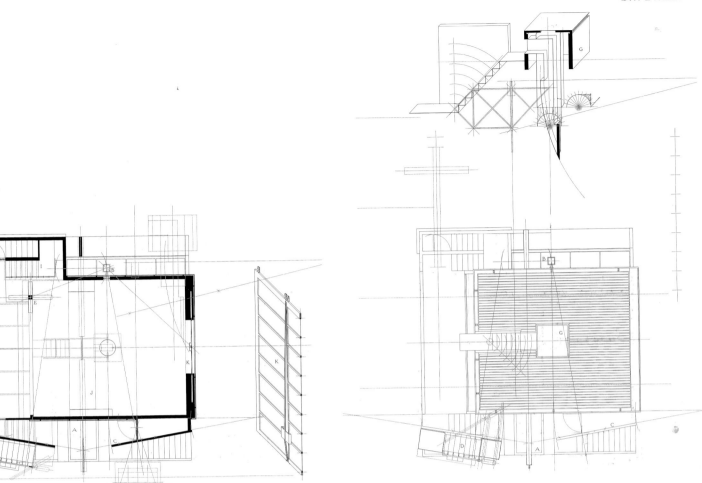

171

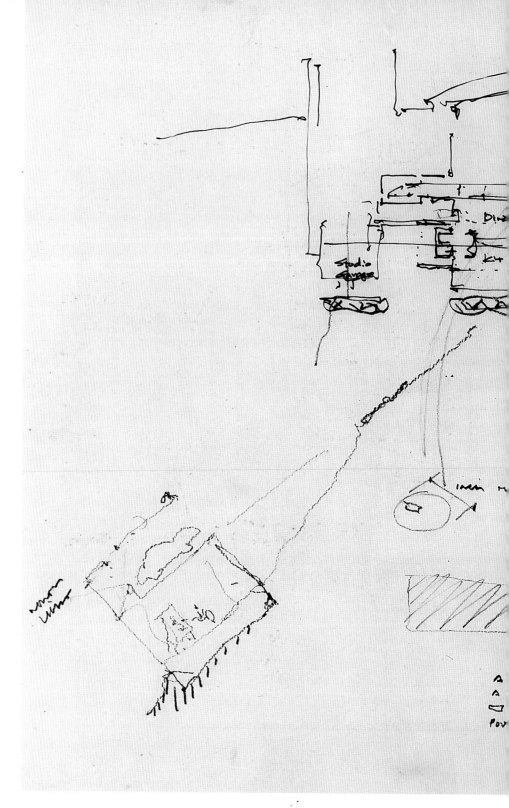

This residence and guest house is on two acres of land overlooking the Pacific Ocean in Montecito, California. The client wanted to utilize the extraordinary topography and views of the city and wished the primary living spaces of the residence to be on one level adjacent to the upper boundary of the site.

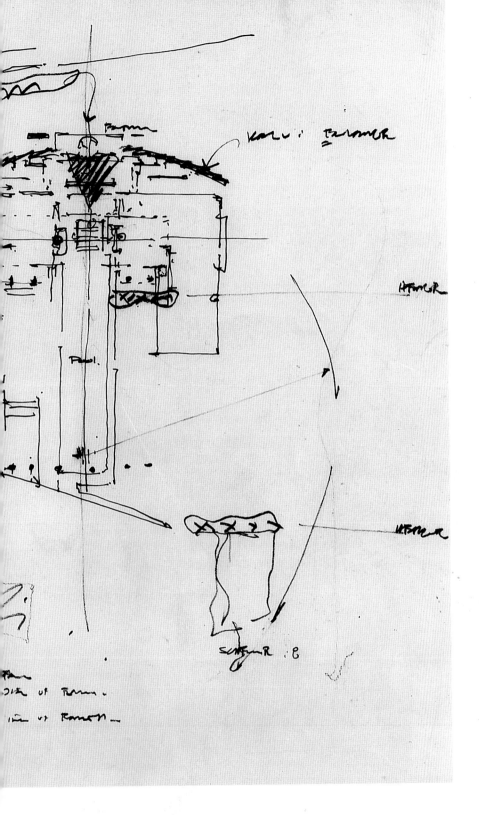

The house has been created out of three organizational systems. A primary orientation along the cardinal points of the compass has been subsumed by two other geometries. One is made up of an axis which connects the major entry to the house in the rear to the views of the ocean. This axis is elaborated in a series of linear progressions of solids and voids that run perpendicular to it. The other is formed by the fragments of a circular wall. While the first "Mercator" orientation is meant to imply global connections, the entry axis localizes the house in terms of the immediate context and then works out this specific orientation in the linear progressions. The wall, finally, calls forth notions of private ownership and territory.

These geometries together create a house made up of totemic pylons constructed of concrete, exposed steel T-frame structures, and walls of stucco and redwood. The progression of these solid elements is reversed in the character of the negative spaces. Ultimately, the relationship between center and periphery is inverted, forcing the life of the house to the periphery, where it comes into contact with those issues of site, context and connection that form the underlying pattern of the project.

174

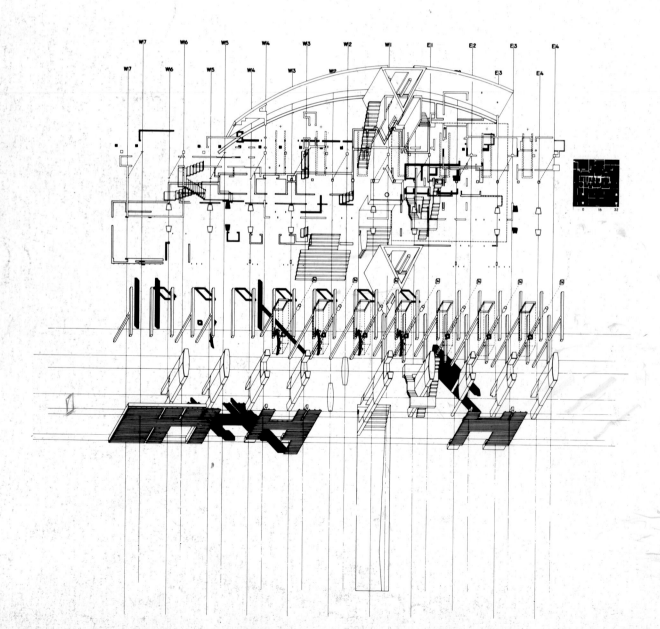

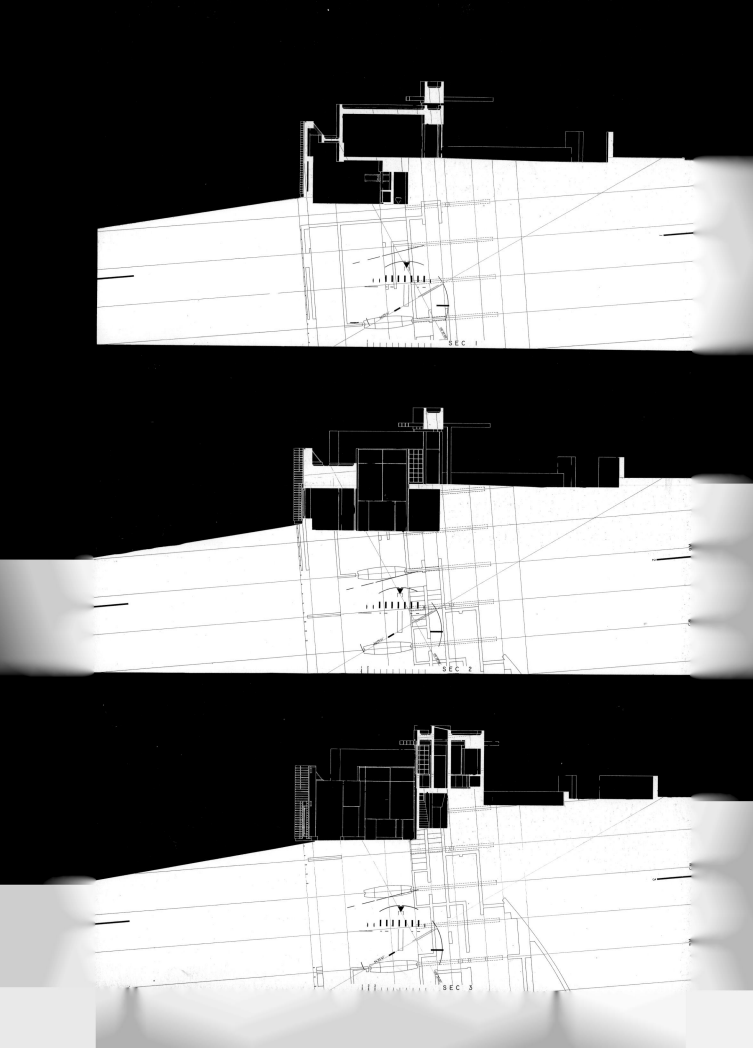

SEC 1

SEC 2

SEC 3

SEC 4

SEC 5

SEC 6

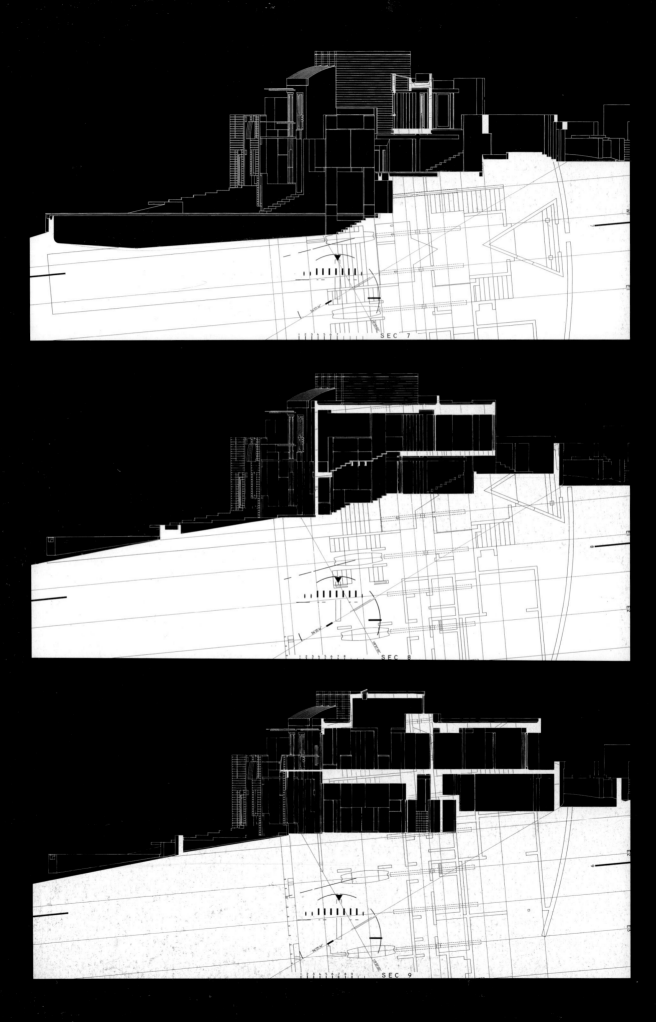

SEC 7

SEC 8

SEC 9

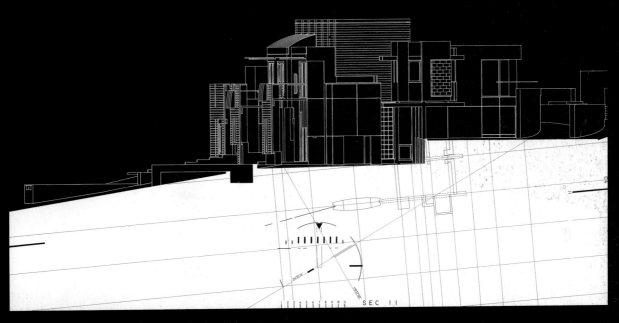

SEC 10

SEC 11

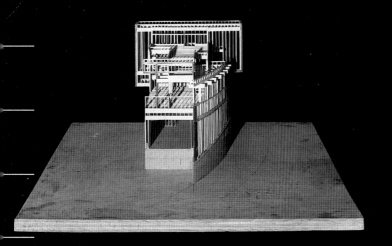

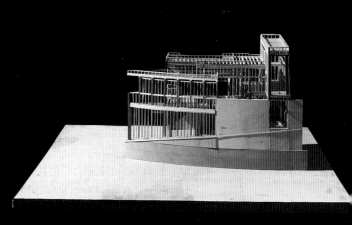

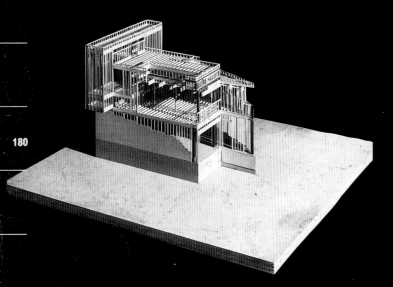

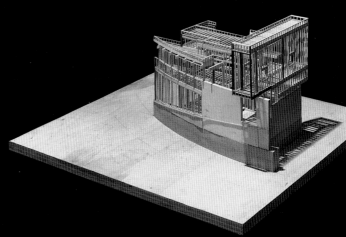

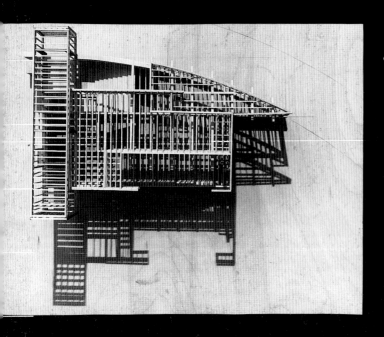

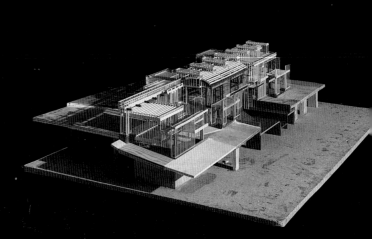

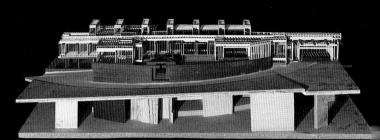

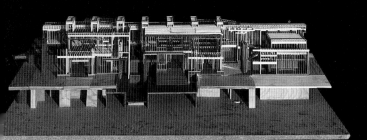

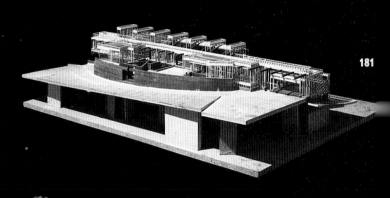

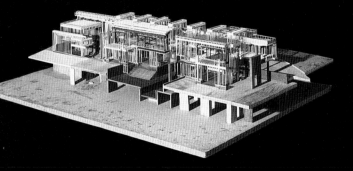

181

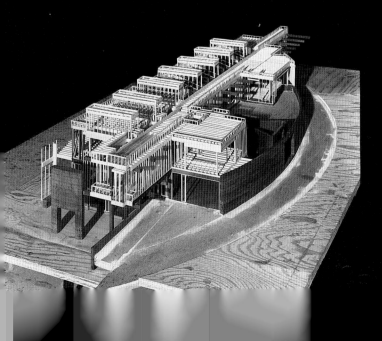

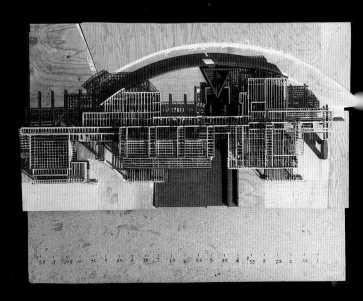

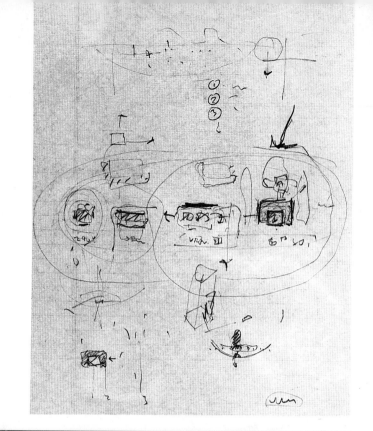

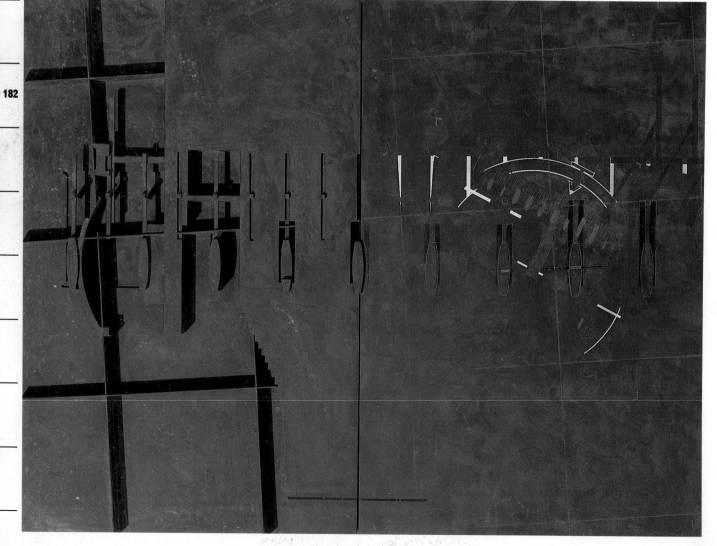

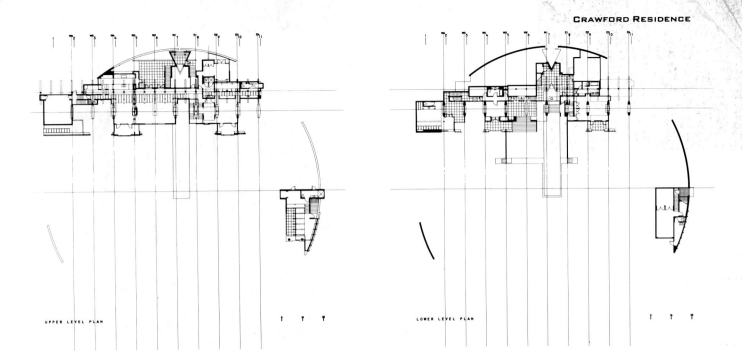

UPPER LEVEL PLAN

LOWER LEVEL PLAN

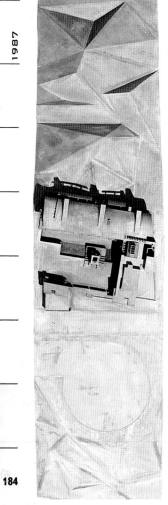

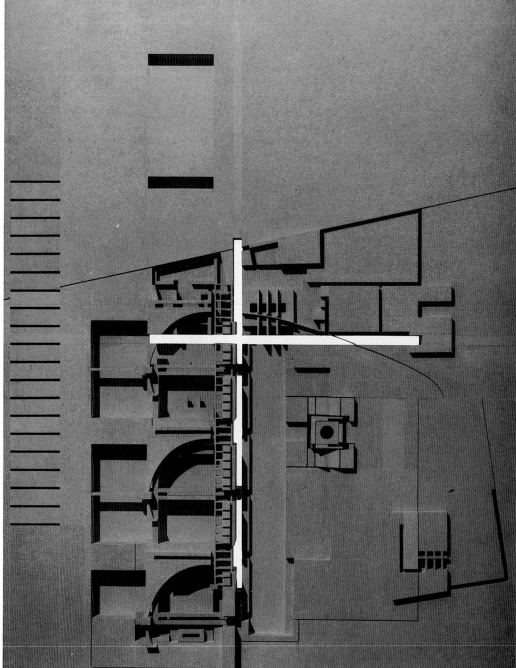

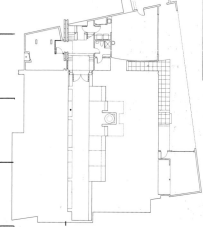

This contemporary fortress on a hill outside of Reno, Nevada was designed for a single businessman who anticipates a future family. The client asked for a house with a strong image when seen from the city. He also wanted a connection between the bedroom area and the pool, since he begins and ends each day by swimming, and a wine cellar and a secret room.

The site is in part of the Great Basin Desert. The landscape of this largest desert in America is bleak and otherworldly. The earth, colored in varying hues and rising to jagged mountains, is in the process of pulling apart, breaking the crust apart into giant blocks which form island-like habitats or mesas between the valley floors. This house looks down from one of these mesas onto the gridded oasis of Reno. The intention of this design was to describe the physical characteristics of the land and the properties of the soil in order to decode the natural phenomena of the environment.

The site is bounded by an external and indefinite edge: part of the "site" jumps into the building, and the house is extended onto the site. The material of the site is the material of the building: sand and gravel from the vicinity are used to make the concrete and block of the new construction. There are three parts to the house. The first is a definite boundary, which makes the house into a compound. The second is a geometry based on the cardinal points and on the city grid below. Defined by two massive concrete walls, twenty feet high and two feet thick, the geometry is independent of the programmatic and spatial volumes. Finally, there is the curved wood and copper roof which contains and defines all of those spaces. By registering the wall geometry selectively in the functional elements of the house, we created a relationship between an abstract ordering system and the idiosyncrasies of daily activities.

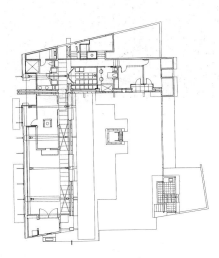

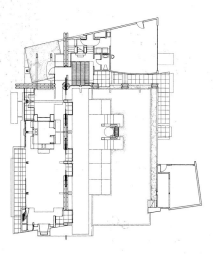

ELÉVATION N

100.

— 7.0.
—11.6.

ELEVATION S

— 12.6
— 10.0

—10.0

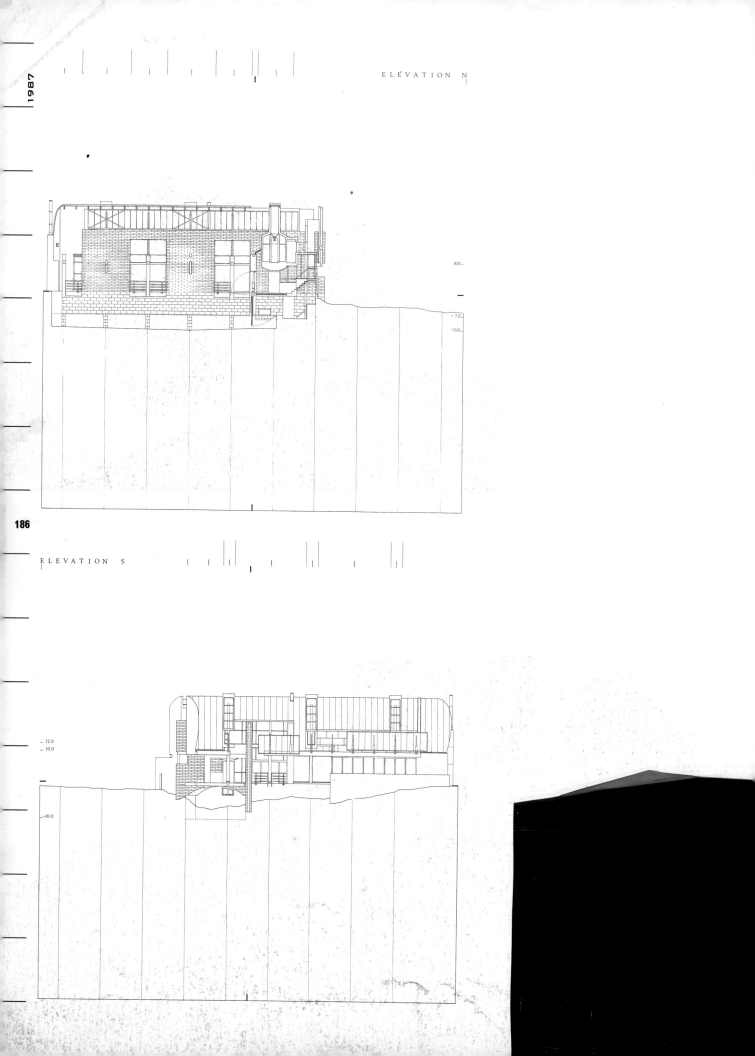

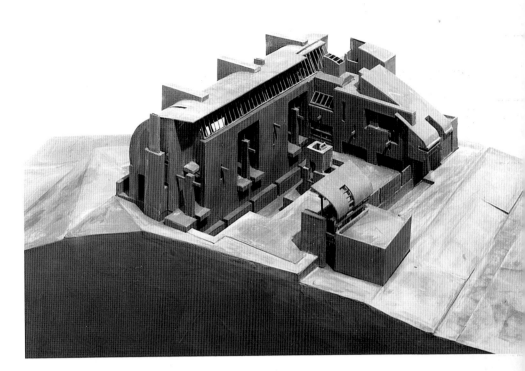

187

ISOMETRIC

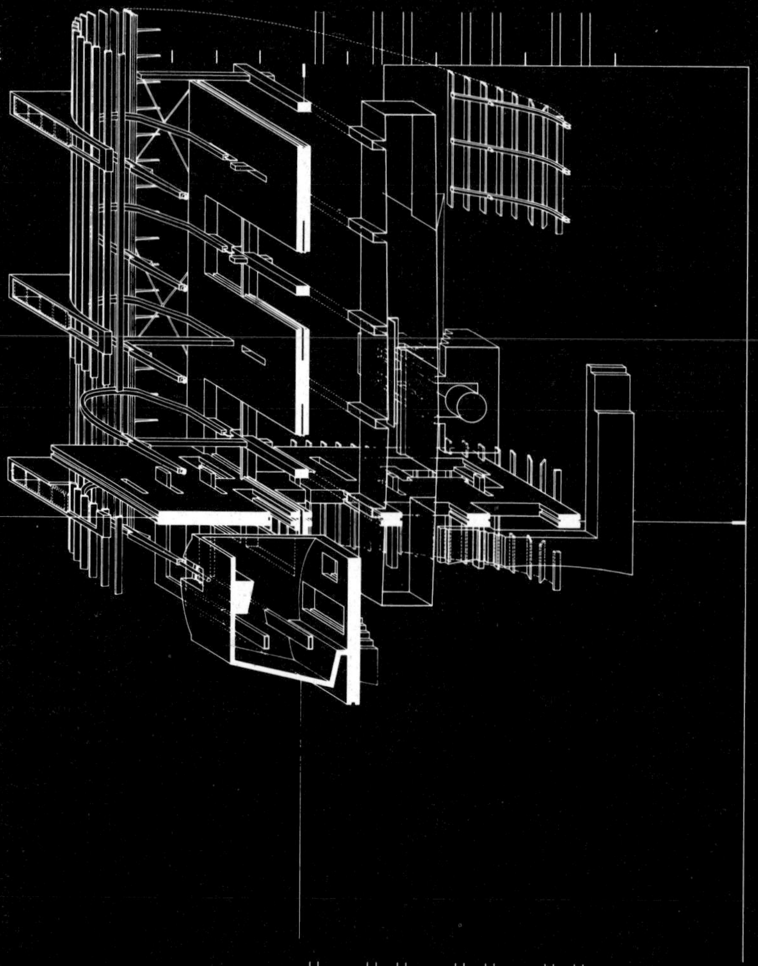

188

ISOMETRIC

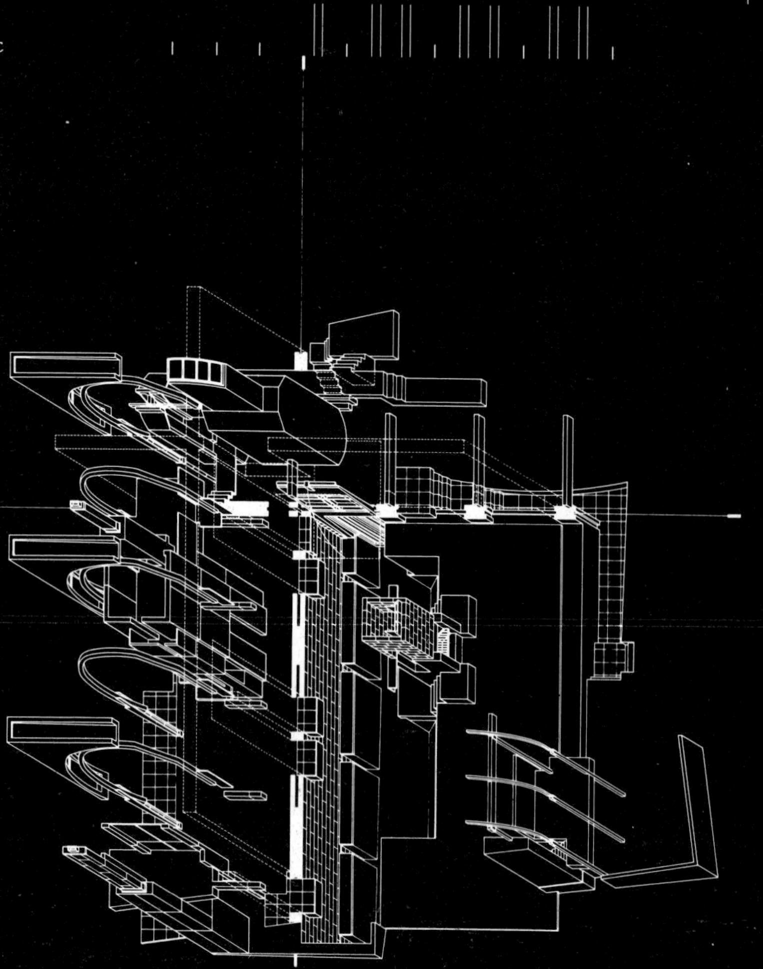

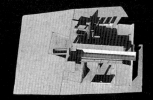

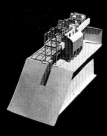

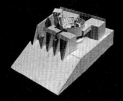

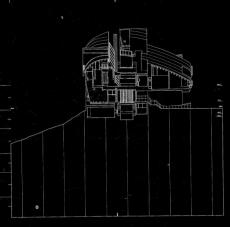

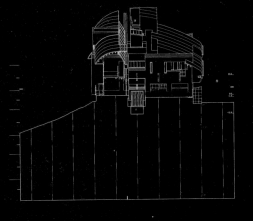

SECTION 4

SECTION 2

SECTION 3

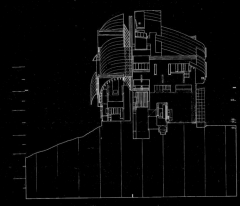

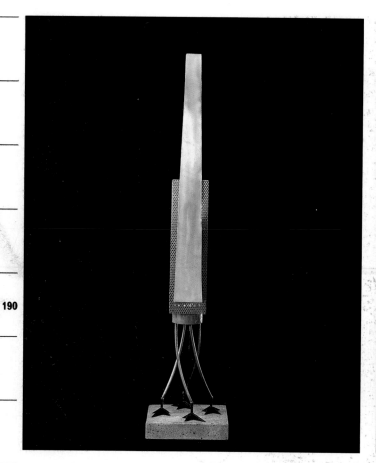

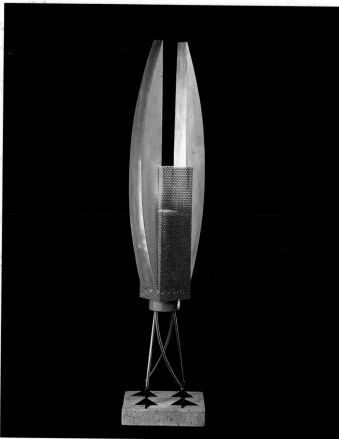

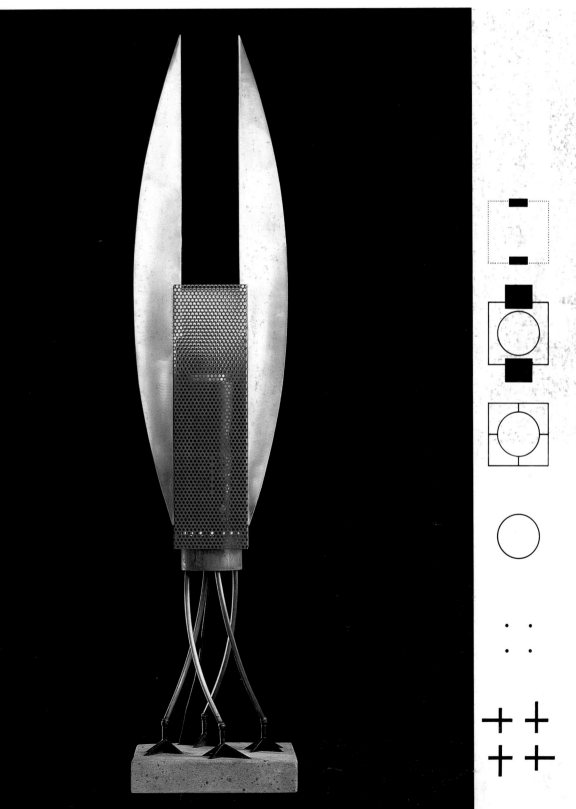

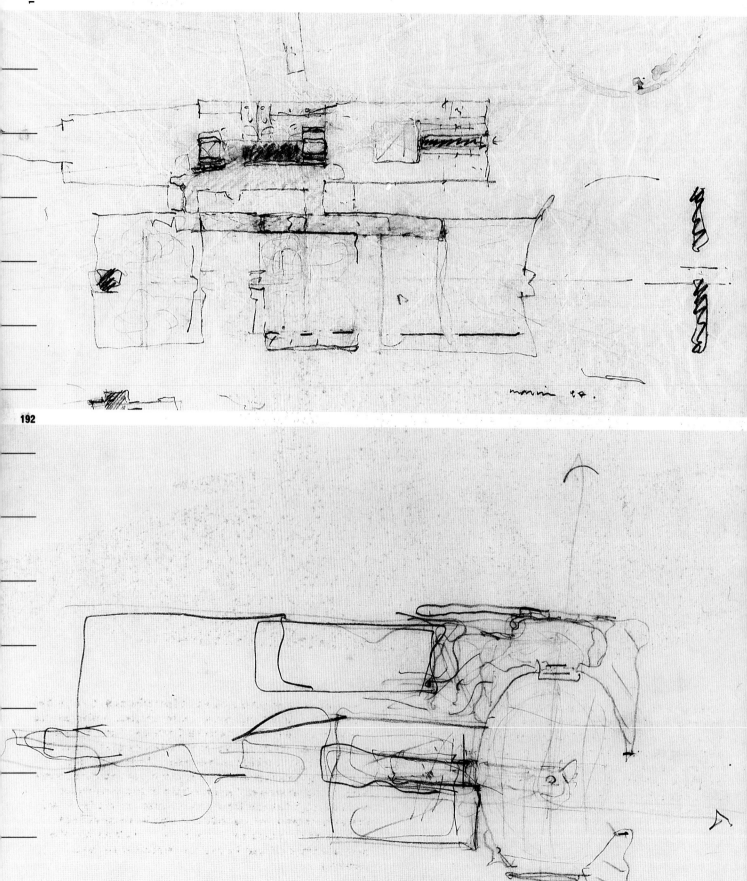

Malibu
Beach House

This house has been placed on a long and narrow site facing the Pacific Ocean on one side and a major highway on the other. The site has been split into two parts, and a separate building has been placed on each half. The "house" facing the ocean is informed by the properties of the ocean and is diagramed as a wave. The rear "house" is entrenched and vertical, serving as a mooring for the first building. Both structures exhibit a mechanical repetitiveness, calling up the continuous motion of waves following one another towards the shore.

The two halves are connected by a horizontal plane that marks the upper limit of the building volume. Garage, storage and service space, a maid's room and a bathroom form the common lower level. On the main floor, a living and dining area, kitchen, and library, as well as a formal entry, are layered from the ocean to the road, while bedrooms are placed on the upper level. The sequence of spaces makes use of the linear character of the site and is accentuated by fragments of walls that start a rhythm at the formal entry and continue through the house. The wood frame is placed on wood pilings and concrete grade beams and slab, and clad with granite. Weight has been made a function of the material used, even when the materials themselves seem to be stripped of mass. The project is meant to be perceived as permanent.

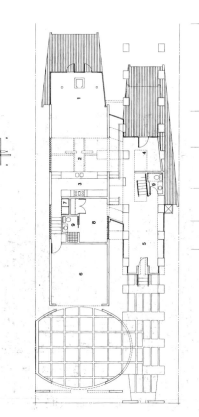

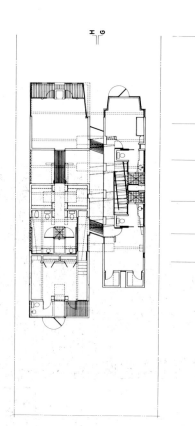

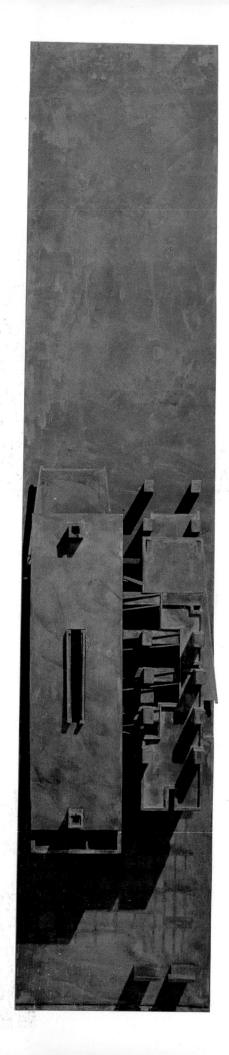

A

B

C

D

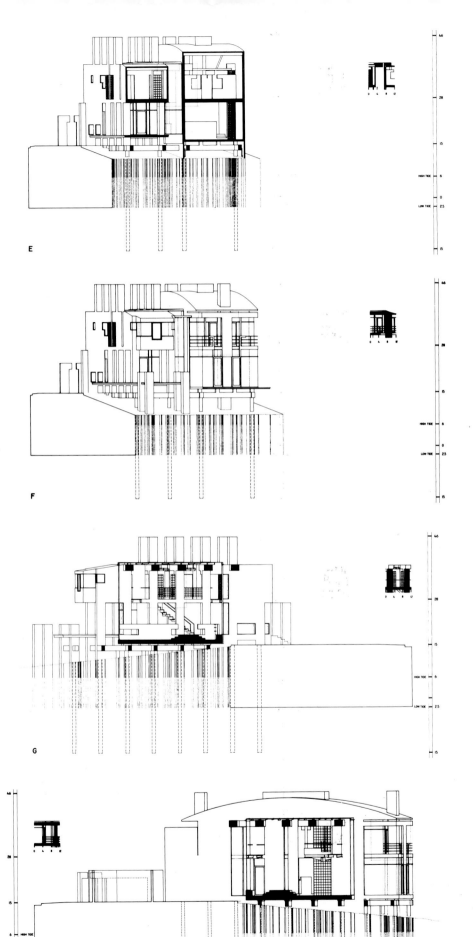

E

F

G

H

1988

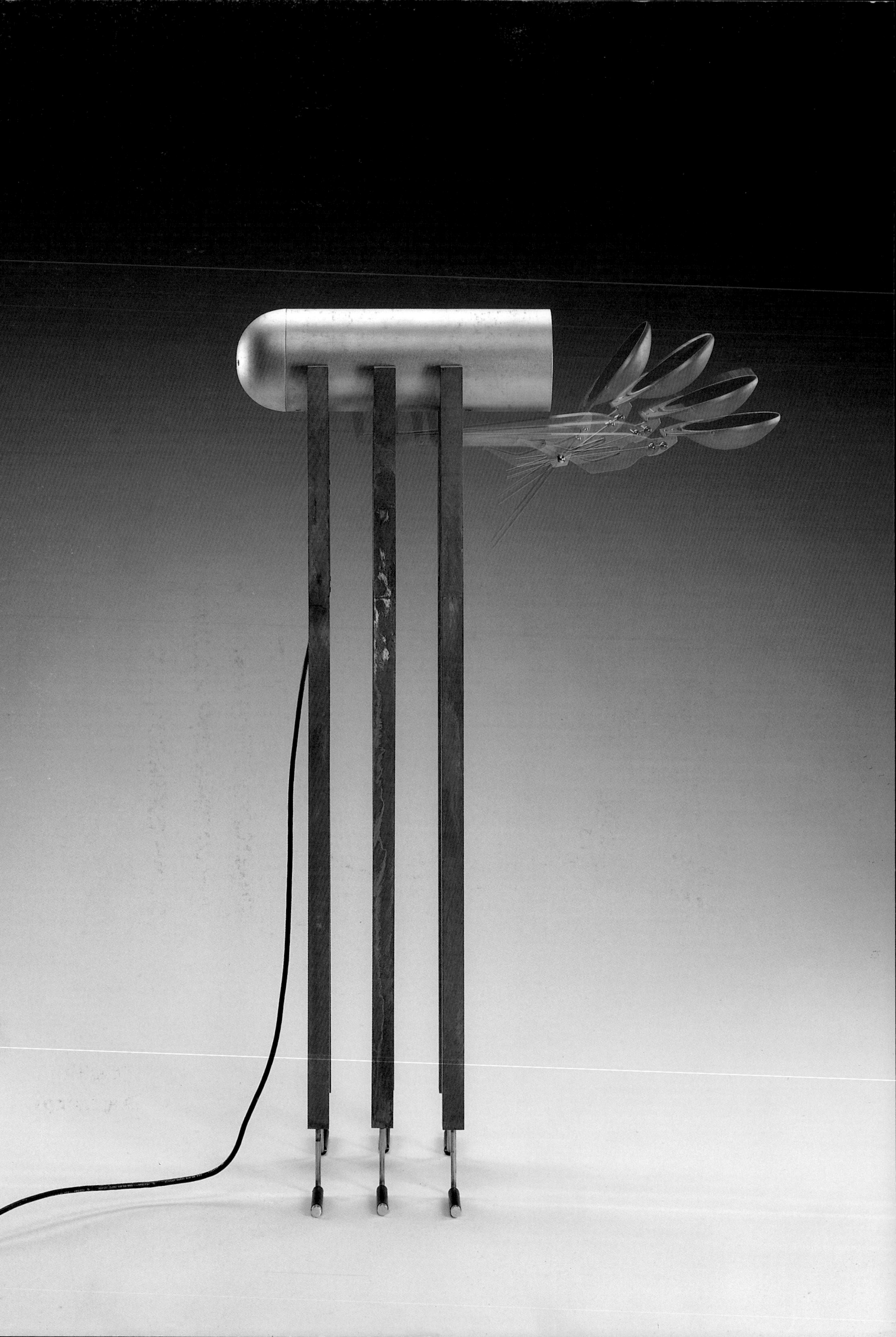

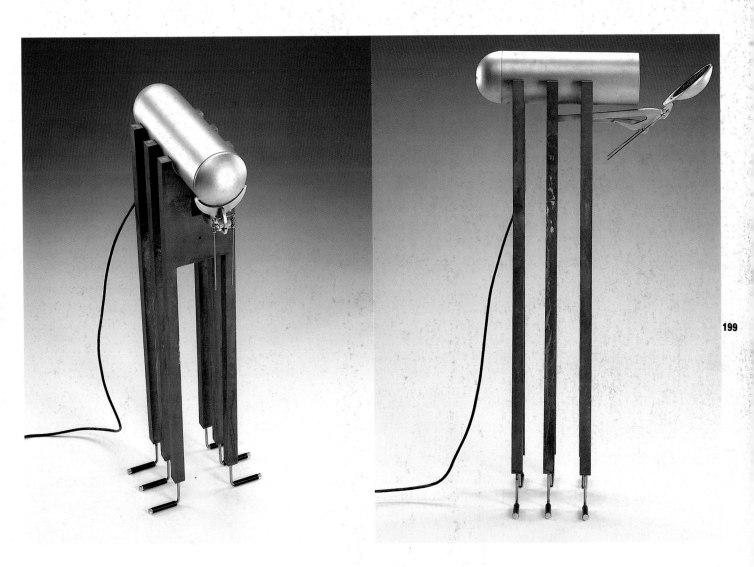

199

(Barking
Dog Lamp)

The 32 by 109 inch glass top of this table is supported by steel stabilizer bars which allow the table to respond to pressure when one leans on the top. In designing this table, we assumed that notions emanating from police battering rams and from high performance automobiles could be translated into a horizontal surface. The table embodies balance, risk, tension, entomorphism, ephemerality and obsolescence.

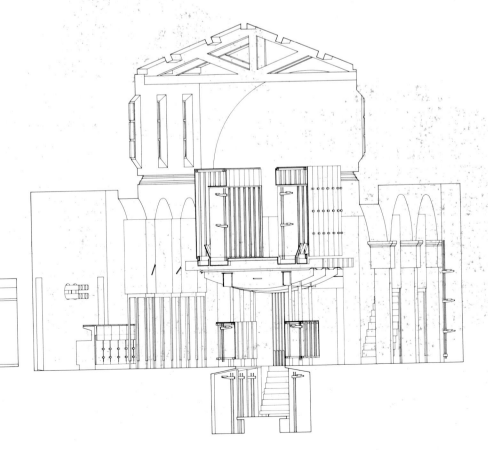

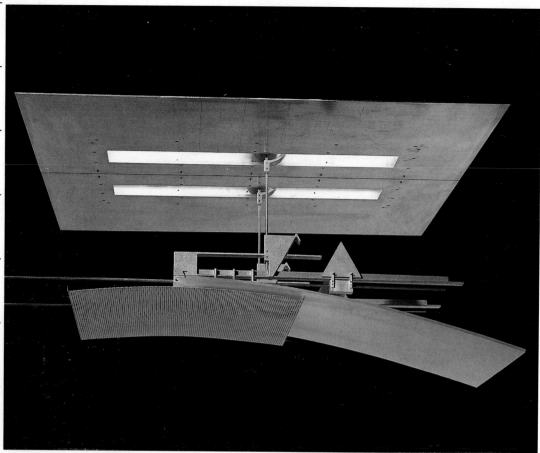

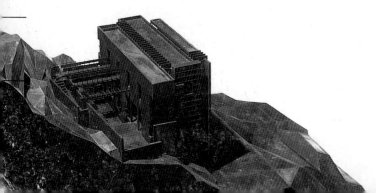

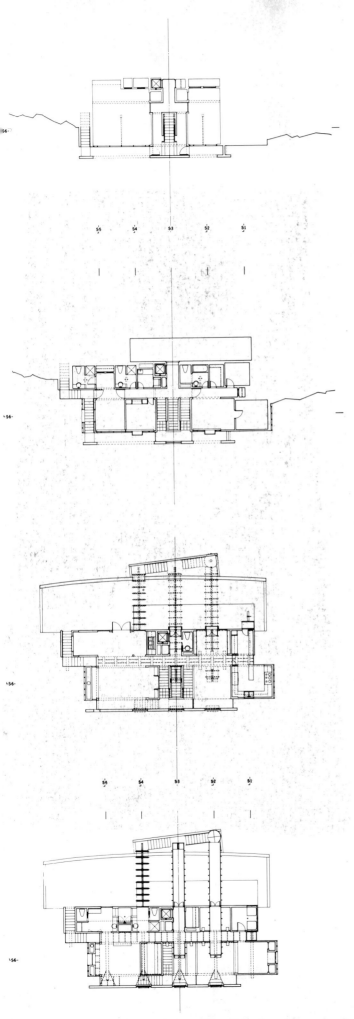

This 4,600 sq.ft. house is on an almost unbuildable half-acre of steeply sloping land in the Los Angeles foothills. The functions have been stacked vertically, starting with the garage and moving up from bedrooms and a studio to the living and dining room, while the master bedroom and study are on the top floor.

The site dictated the use of thick walls. These stucco and aluminum cast panel-clad walls are then layered, and describe the boundaries of the house, thus making evident the "force" of the site. A series of elongated boundaries pierce the bridges. One can thus move parallel to the built forces of the house and experience the views made possible by the construction. A vertical axis, made up of an entry volume and vertical circulation areas, finally ties together all functions to the entry and the view. It is by moving into and through the house along this axis that one sees revealed the various conditions that define the tectonics of the house.

211

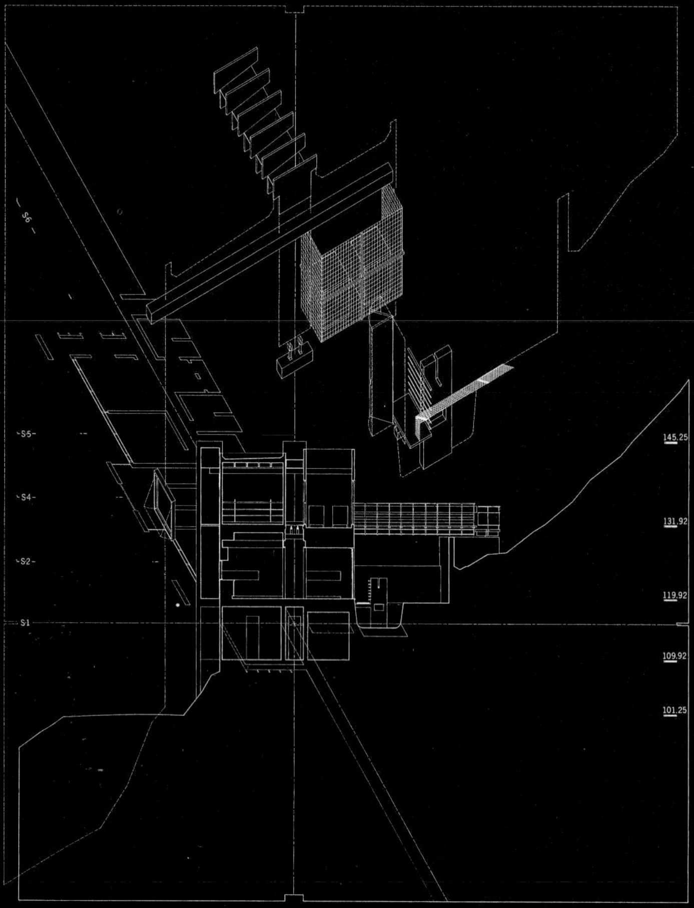
S6
S5
S4
S2
S1
145,25
131,92
119,92
109,92
101,25

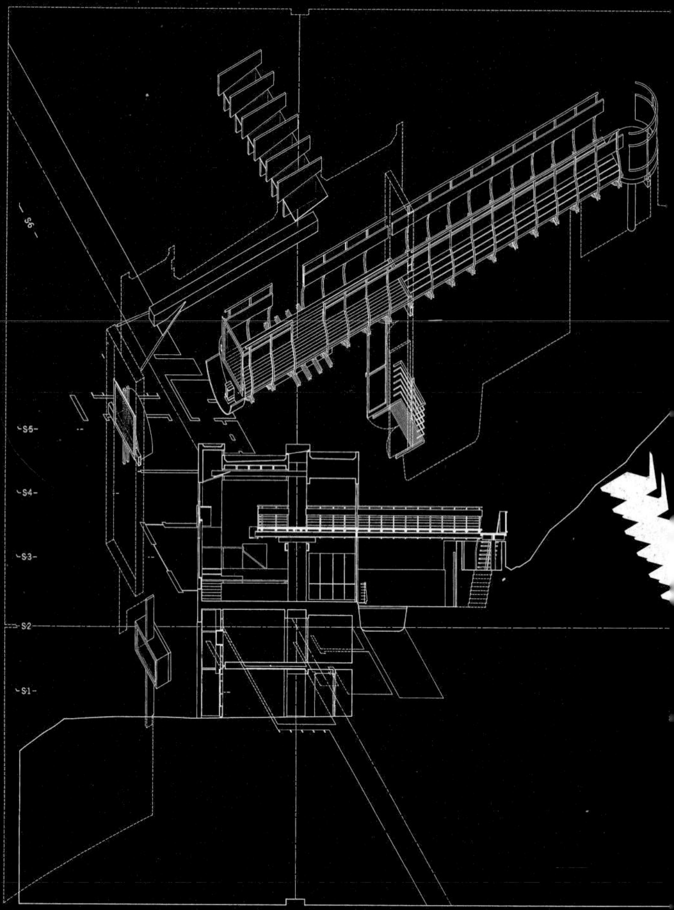
S6
S5
S4
S3
S2
S1

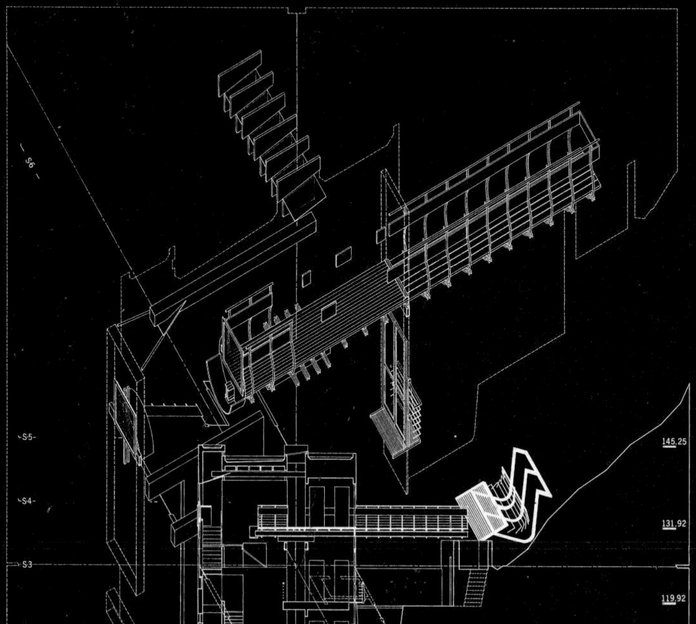
S6
S5
S4
S3
S2
S1
145,25
131,92
119,92
109,92
101,25

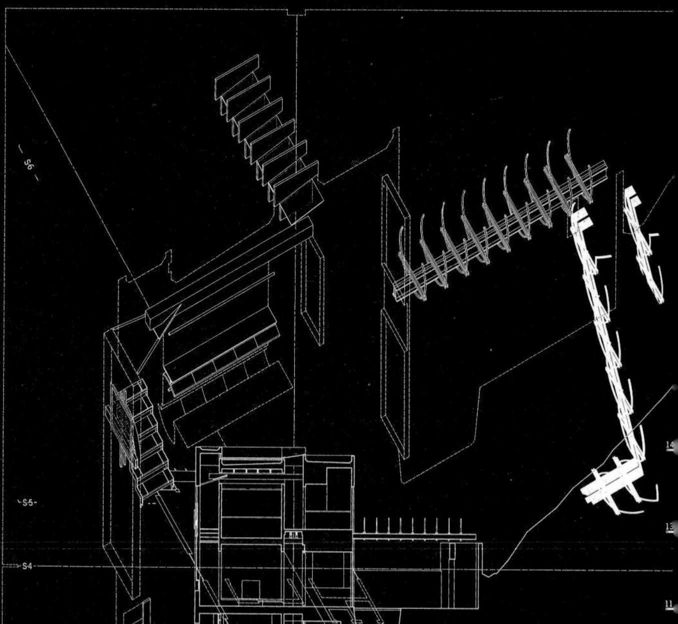
S6
S5
S4
S3
S2
S1

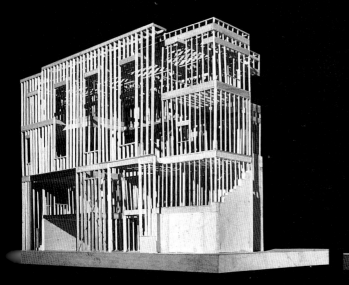

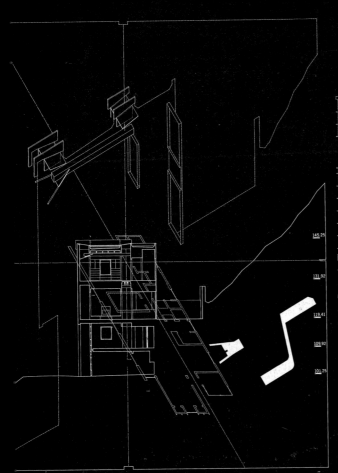

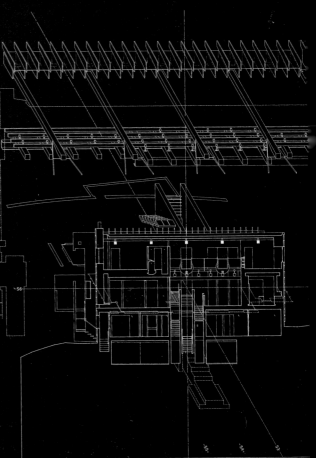

145.25

131.92

119.41

109.92

101.25

S6

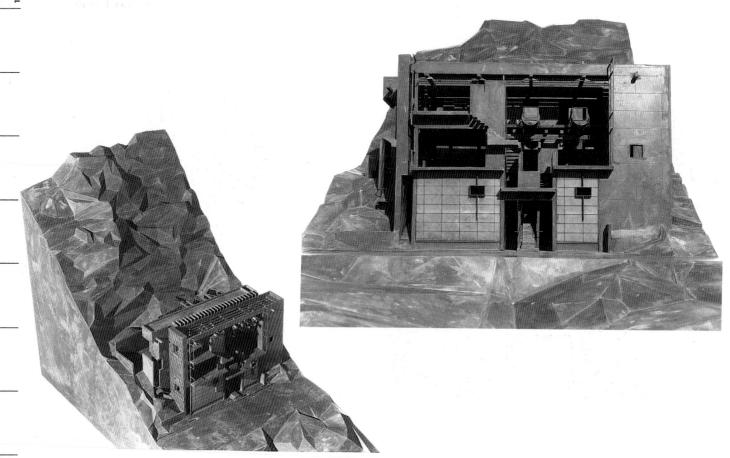

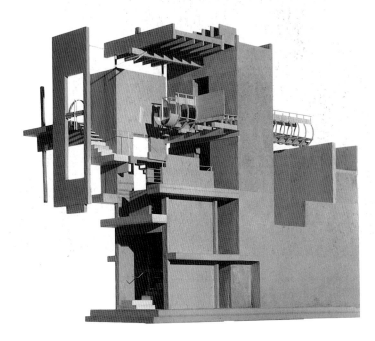
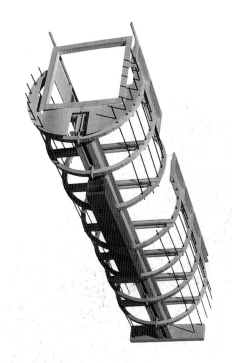

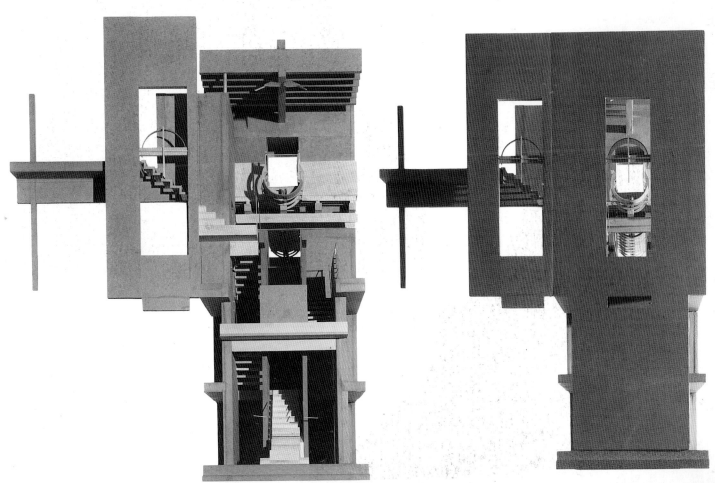

216

Vecta

Six luminescent containers, conceived to be *objects* in and of themselves, allow for voyeuristic, fragmentary glimpses of six chairs displayed within them. These radiant objects organize the interior space they share to establish a sense of place—both permanent and ephemeral.

The project was conceived as a travelling installation at two large trade fairs for furniture marketed in showrooms in New York and Los Angeles. Given the problem of finding a way to display 50 chairs in a convention center showing perhaps thousands of other objects, our decision was to choose only six of them, and then create interest through mystification by hiding the chairs within an object. The fragments of chairs one is able to see are revealed within the layered or hidden space and its light.

A lone beautiful woman obscured by her veil engages our attention even as she is surrounded by so many Emperors in their new clothes.

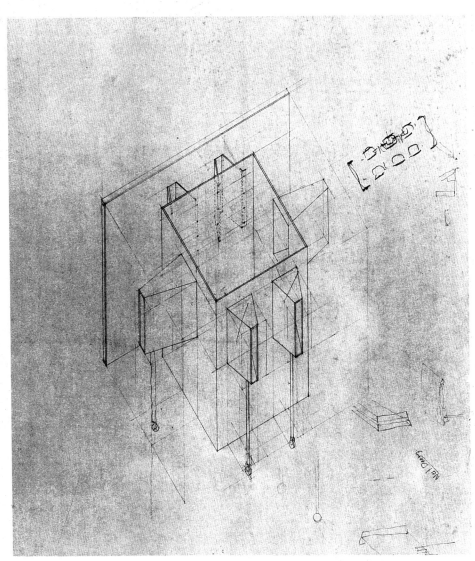

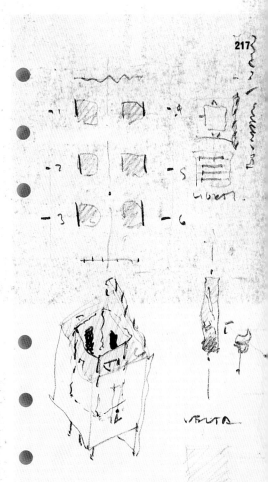

217

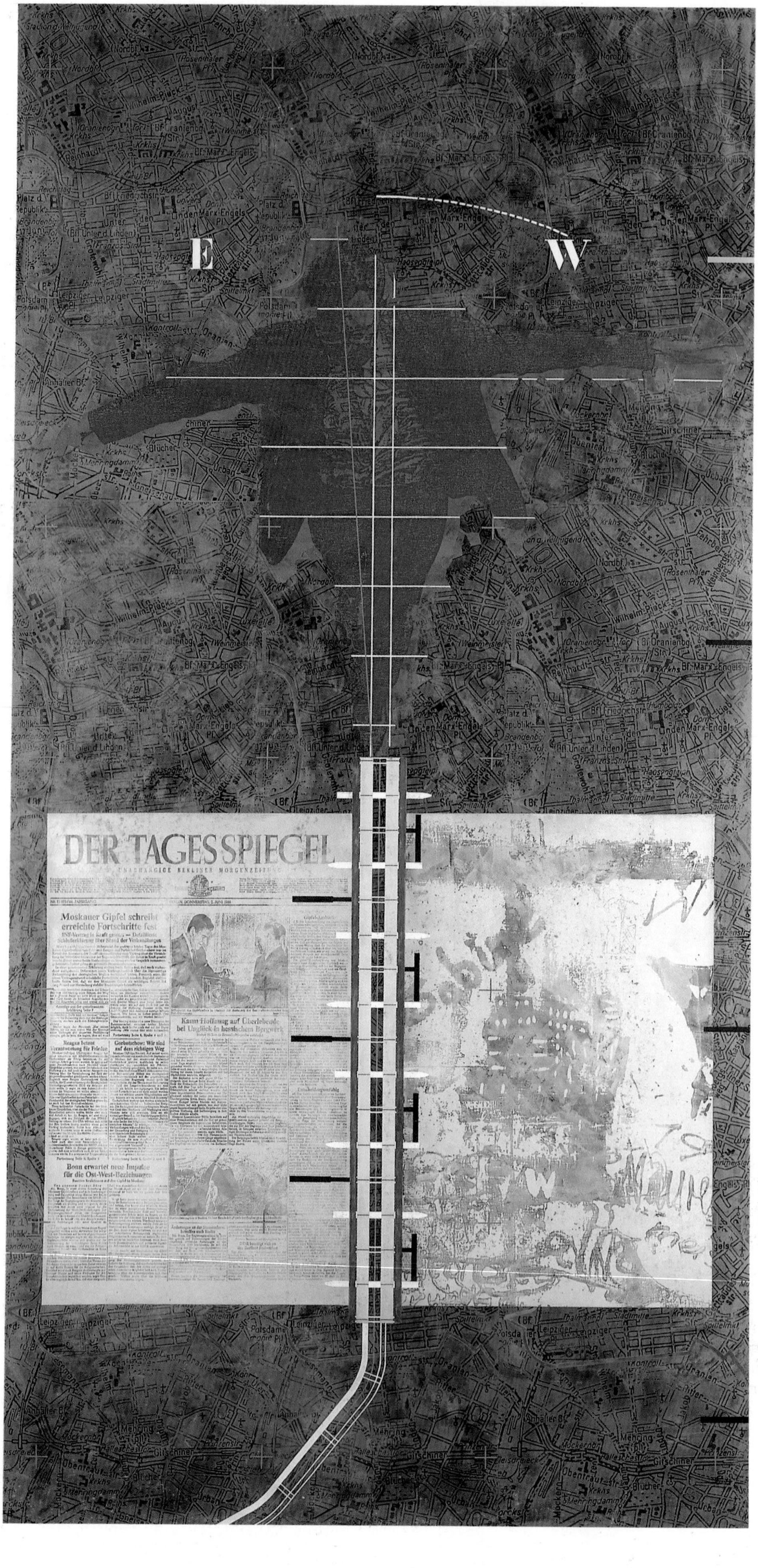
E
W
DER TAGESSPIEGEL
UNABHÄNGIGE BERLINER MORGENZEITUNG
Moskauer Gipfel schreibt erreichte Fortschritte fest
Kaum Hoffnung auf Überlebende bei Unglück in hessischem Bergwerk
Reagan betont Verantwortung für Frieden
Gorbatschow: Wir sind auf dem richtigen Weg
Bonn erwartet neue Impulse für die Ost-West-Beziehungen

Our interest in the Berlin Wall Project was in the permanent aspects of the political and physical division of the City. We were interested in its meaning to the future population and to the specific East/West political connotation.

Our proposal is a fragment of a new wall, itself an *occupied* zone. The proposed project creates a social conduit encouraging arms length debate and allowing for continuous human interaction. One occupies the space of the wall. Though free to occupy the wall and violate its boundaries, one is ultimately trapped within its confining and proscribed nature. Upon entry one has a sense of breaking rules or of violating accepted political conventions. Easterners pass across the space to the West (Westerners to the East) bridging the datum of the original wall (now a trench—an inverted negative wall). As one moves through the pedestrian walkways, this possibility recurs at regular increments as one is able to move perpendicular to the wall perceiving both East and West and enabling one to experience the city as a whole.

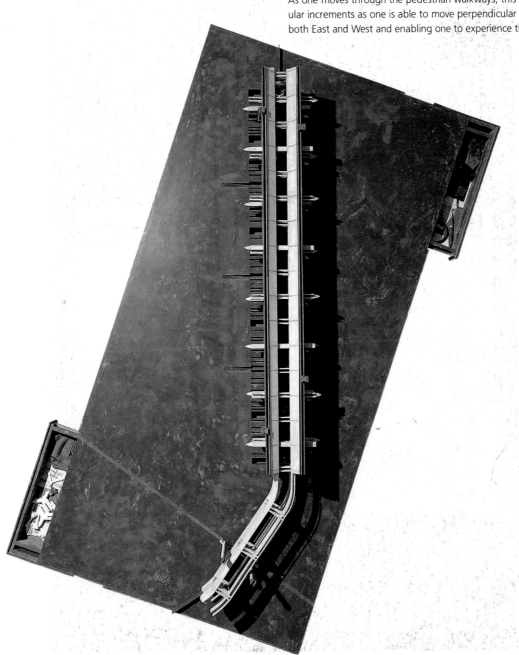

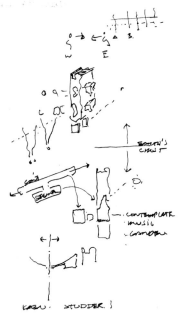

Under the current political circumstances, the project is anticipated to operate as a place for general social/cultural activity, accommodating vendors of all types, musicians, street theater, etc. The project's external surfaces will undergo daily change as artists (West on East and East on West) work continuously.

The project is scaled to reflect its edge condition and its location adjacent to the Brandenburg Gate, and is conceived as an object structure stitching together the Tiergarten (on the West) and the DMZ emptiness (to the East). Our intention is to create a permanent, living monument which will concretize and reconnect the fissure which is the Berlin Wall.

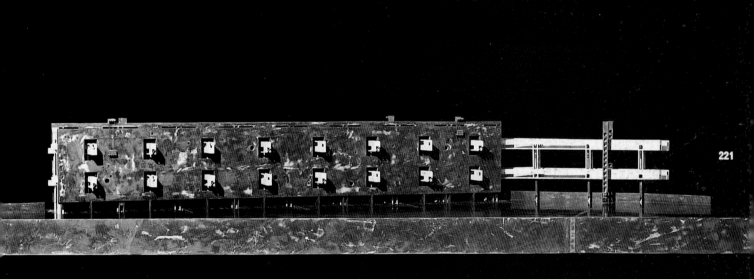

221

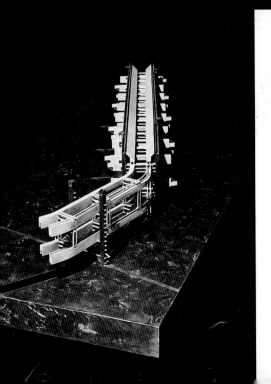

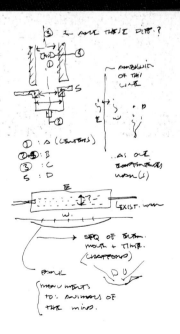

222

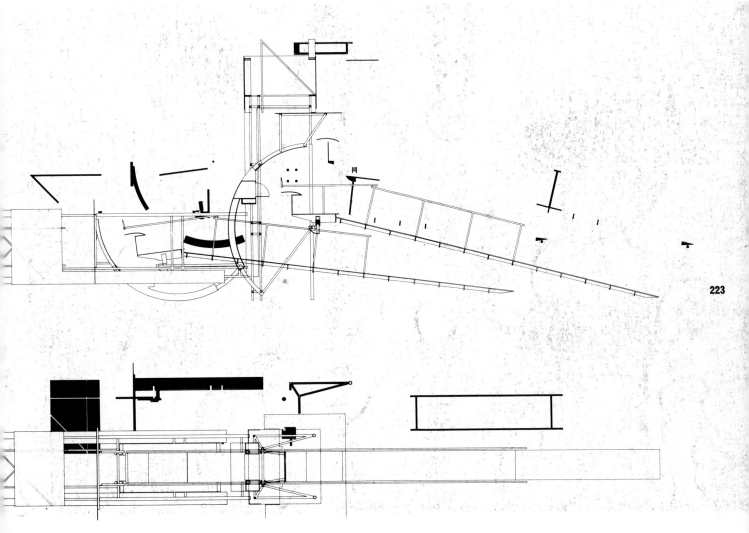

223

The lifeguard tower was produced as an alternative to the existing ones sited incrementally at ¼ mile intervals along the Beach in Santa Monica, California.

The tower responds to the seasonal beach condition which calls for winter storage of these structures to sites adjacent to the beach. A Dragster-like frame rotates 90 degrees from the vertical to the horizontal position, with the ramp functioning as a yoke connected to a tractor. The back surfaces of the towers are now utilized as skids, facilitating movement to the storage lot.

PHOTOS OF THIS & THAT...

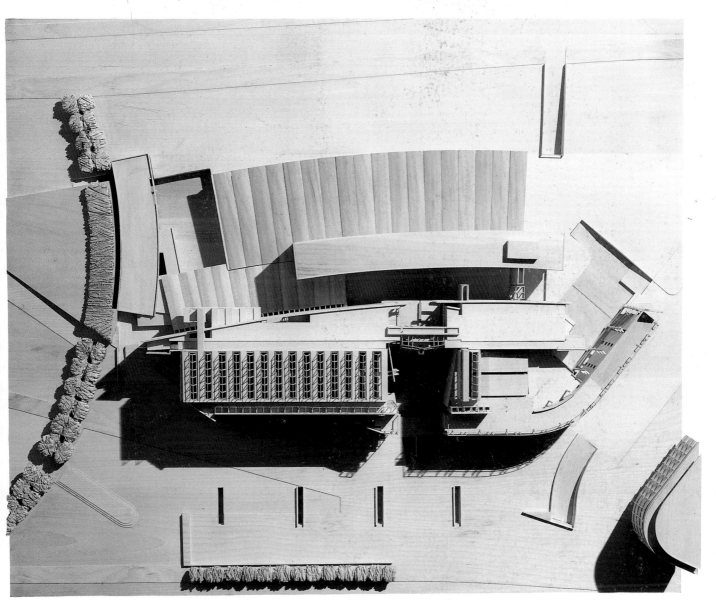

The library addition was designed to be part of an urban ensemble, recognizing the site's importance within the city of Berlin. The intent of our proposal was to develop a library that would hover between figure (object: sacred and honorific) and ground (contextual: profane and accessible). The idea was generated outward from an idealized core to the specificity of program and site. The core had two parts: a solid (the open access areas of the main public reading room), and a void (the courtyard responding to the "force" of the Friedrichstrasse axis, maintaining its historic continuity despite the existence of the Wall). The positioning of the new complex was intended simultaneously to reinforce and reinterpret the original architectural strategy, it consequently could have been read as a single building. The peripheral parts of the new project were concerned with connection and definition. Our goals were to 1) open the line of axis at Mehringplats, 2) make Blucherplatz a space compatible with the new complex, 3) de-scale Blucherstrasse and make an overt connection to the block configuration of the Hertie Department Store, 4) formulate a strong optical relationship between Blucherplatz and the Church zum Heiligen Kreuz, and 5) maintain the relationship between the garden, the existing reading room, and the view to the cemetery from the office block.

The existing park was augmented by fragments of old and new (historical traces and the new project). The major architectural gesture was an arcade of trees (borrowing and reiterating the formal idea of the original library) disposed to define and focus on the physical and social relationship with the Church zum Heiligen Kreuz. The trees extended the geometry of the children's library (literally in the park) which was positioned as a fragment of an earth berm and was open to a private courtyard. Newly defined paths along urban block configurations and fragments of the new building formed places (individual and social); both were intended to make the park transitional.

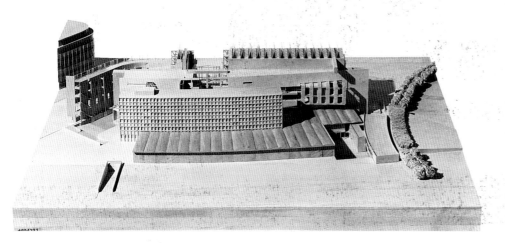

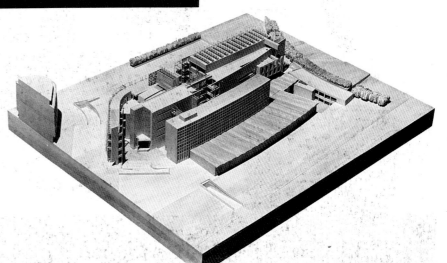

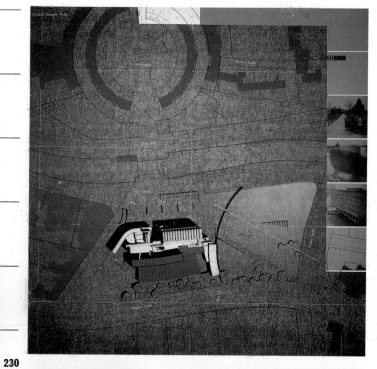

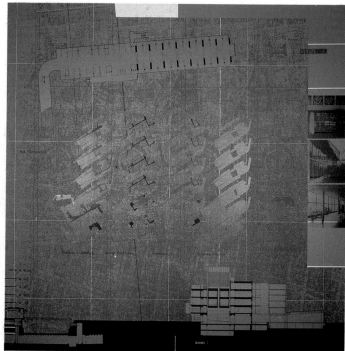

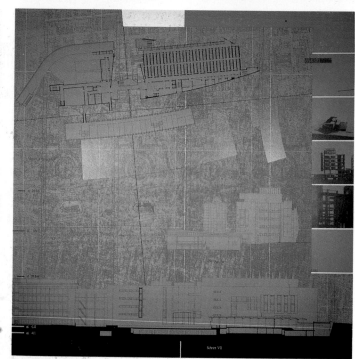

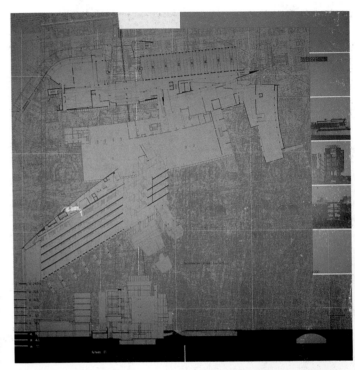

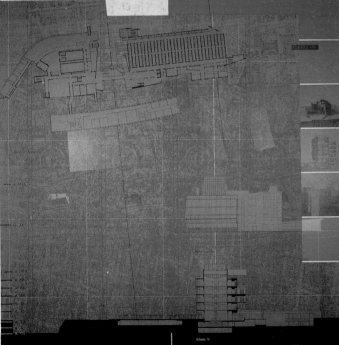

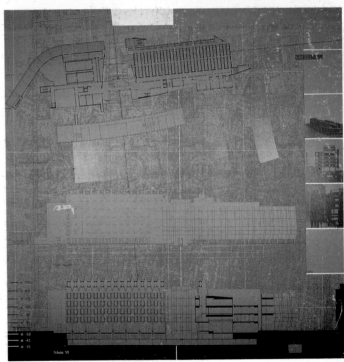

There was a direct relationship between the urban intentions and the internal functioning of the new complex. The proposed addition was to enhance one's comprehension of location and choice of movement within a complex, multi-departmental facility. The new pedestrian circulation system was to be linear and perpendicular to the Friedrichstrasse axis; it was predicated on one's perception of the court's formal termination of Friedrichstrasse. The entrance was to have been on the western edge of this court and was accessed via Blucherplatz, the two-story arcade defining Blucherstrasse, or the stairwell connecting the proposed new subterranean public parking.

232

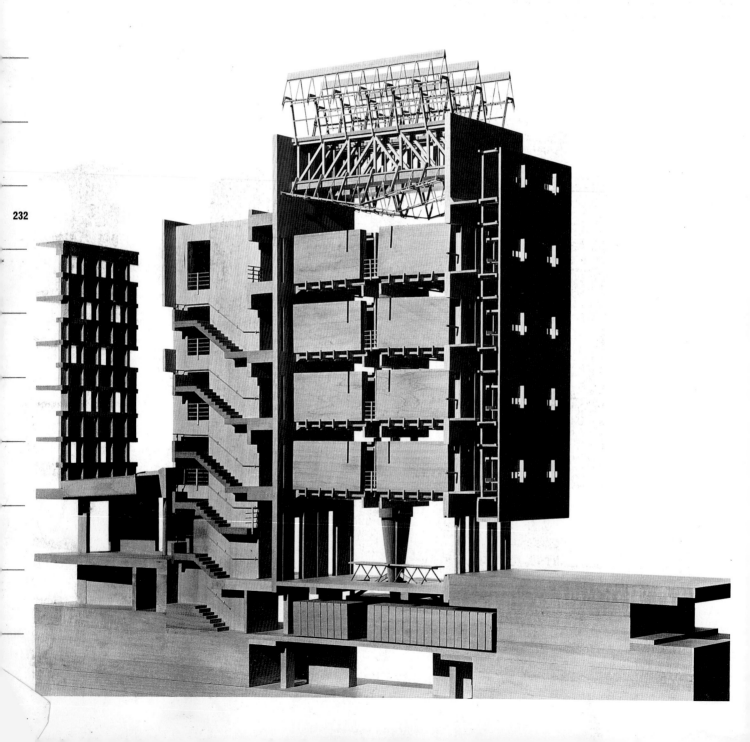

The major new space of the library (its core) was designed to be a "cathedral of knowledge." Suspended rooms, composed of four departments stacked vertically, made up the upper volume of this space. A light-gathering roof and the solid/void nature of this organization allowed light to filter through to the ground plane on which is located the main reading room. Tables which are used for the display of new books form a solid "ceiling" for a skylight which reveals the structure of the building, undermines the solidity of the floor, and allows perception of the closed stacks within the subterranean level.

The north boundary (The Blucherplatz Façade) of the open stacks was made up of individual carrels (fragments of rooms, each with a desk and an operable window). The south boundary was flanked by all other ancillary functions organized around the central elevators. Within this zone were small group-study rooms that also accommodated more books. Additional non-programmed reading and study areas throughout the building, on landings with prime site locations, further expanded communication.

The new building was designed to be made of concrete, except for the book storage section, which would have been of steel. Exterior surfaces were curtain-wall or concrete panels, with the exception of the Blucherplatz façade, which would have been stone or, possibly, stainless steel. Interior finishes would have been steel, plaster, and wood.

233

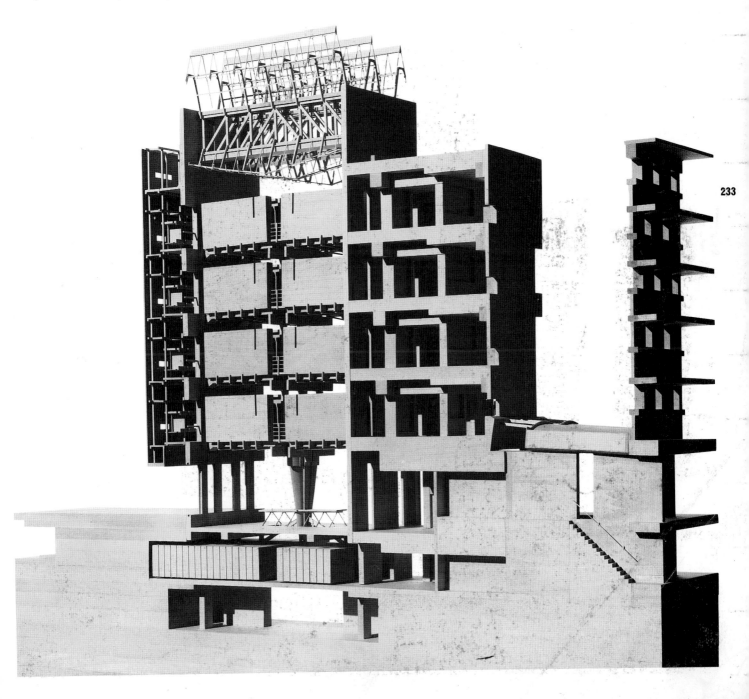

234

CCAIA Award, 1989, Cedar Sinai—Comprehensive
Cancer Center—Award of Merit

AIA award, 1988, Cedar Sinai—Comprehensive Cancer Center—Award of Merit

CCAIA Award, 1988, Kate Mantilini
Restaurant—Award of Merit

National AIA Award, 1988, Kate Mantilini
Restaurant—Honor Award

Progressive Architecture Award, 1988—6th Street
Residence—Citation

Progressive Architecture Award, 1987 Kate Mantilini
Restaurant—Award

Progressive Architecture Award, 1987 Prototypical
Hamburger Stand—Citation

Progressive Architecture Award, 1987 Comprehensive Cancer Center—Citation

AIA Award, 1987, 6th Street Residence—Award of
Honor

AIA Award, 1987, Kate Mantilini Restaurant—Award
of Merit

AIA Award, 1986, Angeli Restaurant—Award of
Merit

National AIA Award, 1986 Bergren Residence—
Honor Award

CCAIA Award, 1986 Bergren Residence—Award of
Merit

CCAIA Award, 1986 72 Market Street—Award of
Merit

AIA Award, 1985 72 Market Street—Award of Merit

AIA Award, 1985, Lawrence Residence—Award of
Merit

AIA Award, 1985, Bergren Residence—Award of
Merit

Progressive Architecture Award, 1985
Venice III House, Bergren Residence—Citation

Progressive Architecture Award, 1984 Hermosa
Beach Commercial Center—Citation

Progressive Architecture Award, 1982—Citation
Western-Melrose Office Building

AIA Award, 1981, Sedlak House—Award

Progressive Architecture Award, 1980 Flores
Residence—Citation

Sacramento Energy Efficient Office Bldg. Competition, Honor Award, 1977—Citation

Progressive Architecture Award, 1977 Riedel Medical Building—Citation

Progressive Architecture Award, 1974 Sequoyah
Educational Research Center—Citation

Gallery of Architecture, Los Angeles, California, "Tangents and Outtakes," July 1–August 12, 1989

Contemporary Arts Center, Cincinnati, Ohio, "Recent Work," July 20–September 1, 1989

Arts Park Performing Arts Pavilion, The Cultural Foundation, Woodland Hills, California, June 5–July 31, 1989

Architects Houses, Deutsches Architektur Museum, Frankfurt, West Germany, September 1– November 26, 1989

University of California, Los Angeles, California, "Recent Work," 1989

Walker Arts Center, Minneapolis, Minnesota, "Three Houses," May 14, 1989–April 28, 1989

Cheney Cowles Museum, Spokane, Washington, "Recent Work," April 12, 1989–June 10, 1989

Harvard University, Cambridge, Massachusetts, "Morphosis," November 15, 1988

Kirsten Kiser Gallery, Los Angeles, California, "Modeling Paste Drawings," 1989

Gallery of Functional Art, Santa Monica, California, January 7, 1989–March 6, 1989

Visual Arts Ontario, R.C. Harris Water Filtration Plant, Toronto, Canada, June 22, 1988–Sept. 30, 1988

Kirsten Kiser Gallery, Los Angeles, California, "California, Lifeguard Towers," July 8–Aug. 13, 1988

2 AES Gallery, Art and Architecture Exhibition Space, San Francisco, California, Sept. 15–Nov. 17, 1988

Aedes Galerie fur Architektur und Raum, Berlin, West Germany, "Berlin–Denkmal oder Denkmodell," Sept. 2–Dec. 2, 1988

National Academy of Design, New York, New York, "The Experimental Tradition: Twenty-five Years of American Architecture Competitions 1960– 1985 (Vietnam Veterans Memorial)," May 16, 1988–July 31, 1988

Cooper-Hewitt Museum, New York, New York, "What Could Have Been: Unbuilt Architecture of the '80s," July 19–Oct. 23, 1988

Australian Center for Contemporary Art, Victoria, Australia, "Dream Houses," May 19–June 19, 1988

Pacific Design Center, Los Angeles, California, "L. A. Architecture: 12 + 12 An Overview," March 23–March 25, 1988

Axis Gallery, Tokyo, Japan, "In-spiration Lighting Exhibition," February 5–February 15, 1988

G.A. Gallery, Tokyo, Japan, " The Emerging Generation in U.S.A," November 7–December 13, 1987

I.D.C., New York, New York, "Forty Under Forty," October, 1986

Max Protetch Gallery, New York, New York, "Architects for Social Responsibility," May/June, 1986, 1985

G.A. Gallery, Tokyo, Japan, "California, Architecture –Morphosis / Eric Owen Moss," April/May, 1985

California, Museum of Science and Industry, "84/84 Olympic Architects," June/August, 1984

Hotel Biltmore, Los Angeles, California, "Architectural Competitions," May, 1984

Museum of Modern Art, San Francisco, California, "California, Counterpoint," November/December, 1983

National Academy of Design, New York, New York, "California, Counterpoint," July/September, 1983

Architectural Association, London, England, "Los Angeles Now," May, 1983

Columbia University, "American Architecture: Innovation and Tradition," February/March, 1983

Institute of Contemporary Arts, London, England "Drawings by Architects," February/March, 1983

La Jolla Museum of Contemporary Art, La Jolla, California,, "The California Condition," November/ December, 1982

Bernard Jacobson Gallery, Los Angeles, California, "Four Houses: Four Cities," July/August, 1982

Ohio State University Art Gallery, "Artist as Architect/Architect as Artist," March/April 1981

Pennsylvania State University Art Gallery, "New Americans: Issues and Thoughts," 1981

The Architectural Gallery, Venice, California, Selected Projects, November, 1979

CCAIA Exhibit, Newport Beach, California, "New Americans: Issues and Thoughts," Rome, Milan, Venice, June/August, 1979

California, Statewide Exhibit, Sacramento Office Building Competition, 1978

Umwelt Galerie, Stuttgart, "Contemporary American Architecture" (Four Projects), January/ March, 1978

"Sequoyah Educational Research Center," *Progressive Architecture*, January, 1974,
p. 67.

MacMasters, Dan. "Villa Floresta Housing," *Los Angeles Times, Home Magazine*, May, 1976, pp. 42–44.

"Riedel Medical Office Building," *Architecture Interieure-Cree*, July/August, 1977, pp. 50–51.

"Riedel Medical Office Building," *L'Architecture D'Aujourd'Hui*, October, 1977.

"Riedel Medical Office Building," *Progressive Architecture*, January, 1977, p. 58.

"Delmer Residence Addition," *Los Angeles Times, Home Magazine*, May 7, 1978,
pp. 14–15.

"Delmer Residence Addition," *Wet Magazine*, May, 1978.

Franklin, Michael. "Young Los Angeles, Five Projects," *Architecture and Urbanism*, April, 1978, pp. 118–125.

McCoy, Esther. "Everyman's Casa," *Progressive Architecture*, July, 1978, pp. 76–79.

"Architecture Gallery," *Los Angeles Times*, October 17, 1979.

Boissier, Oliver. "Fred Delmer Residence," *Architecture Interieure-Cree*, November/December, 1979.

"Current Los Angeles Projects," *Arquitectura*, September/October, 1979, pp. 58–60.

"Flores Residence," *Los Angeles Herald Examiner*, December 19, 1979.

Mack, Mark. "Flores House," *Archetype*, Autumn, 1979, pp. 6–7.

"Mexico House II," *L'Architecture D'Aujourd'Hui*, December, 1979.

"2-4-6-8 House," *Abitare*, December, 1980, pp. 28–30.

Boissiere, Oliver. "The Young Architects of California," *Domus*, March, 1980, pp. 20–21.

"Flores Residence," *Progressive Architecture*, January, 1980.

Giovannini, Joseph. "Entering the Age of More is More," *Los Angeles Herald Examiner*, September 15, 1980, pp. B1, B5.
"New Westside Story," *Interiors*, December, 1980, pp. 92–93.

Jencks, Charles. "Post Modern Classicism, 2-4-6-8- House," *Architectural Design*, May/June, 1980, pp. 110–113.

"1981 AIA Design Awards," *L.A. Architect*, December, 1981.

Buchanan, Peter. "Five Projects," *Architecture Review*, September, 1981, pp. 163–168.

"California Architecture," *Arts and Architecture*, Fall, 1981.

"Interiors by Architects," *L.A. Architect*, September, 1981.

"New Waves in American Architecture, Six Projects," *GA Houses*, Volume 9, 1981,
pp. 152–173.

Bates, Caroline. "Specialties de la Maison, Verdi Restaurant," *Gourmet*, December, 1982, pp. 8–10, 159–167.

"California Condition," *California Architect*, November, 1982.

"California Condition," *La Jolla Museum Catalog*, November, 1982, pp. 65–69.

Filler, Martin. "Houses New Young Human and Fun," *House and Garden*, February, 1982.

"Four Houses; Four Cities," *Images and Issues*, November/December, 1982.

McCoy, Esther. "Retreats in Venice," *Progressive Architecture*, March, 1982, p. 85.

Slesin, Suzanne. "The California Studio House," No publication given, March 6, 1982, p. 87.
"The Studio House: New Trend Setter from California," *New York Times*, April 8, 1982,
p. C6.

"Verdi Restaurant," *Los Angeles Times*, July 12, 1982.

"Western-Melrose Office Building," *Progressive Architecture*, January, 1982, pp. 139–141.

"Young American Architects," *Space Design*, August, 1982, pp. 15–19.

"California Counterpoint," *Institute for Architecture and Urban Studies*, January, 1983.

"California Counterpoint," *New York Times*, July, 1983.

"Current State of the Arts in L.A. Architecture," *Los Angeles Times*, September, 1983.

"Mexico House II," *Space Design*, January, 1983.

Miller, Nory. "Baby Boom Architects," *Metropolitan Home*, July, 1983, p. 46.

"Residential Works," *Architecture and Urbanism*, September, 1983, pp. 29–48.

"Sedlate, Cohen, 2468, Hermosa," *Los Angeles Now*, April, 1983 pp. 38–40.

Webb, Michael. "Restaurants as Theatre," *Arts and Architecture*, June, 1983, p. 60.

Aaron, Peter. "Standing Out and Fitting In," *House and Garden*, October, 1984,
pp. 182–189.

Doubilet, Susan. "Computers in Architecture," *Progressive Architecture*, May, 1984
pp. 146–149.

Giovannini, Joseph. "New Architecture in Venice, CA," *Real Estate as Art*, July, 1984.

Goolrick, Robert Cooke. "Style Setters: The Architects," *Metropolitan Home* May, 1984, p. 79.

"Hermosa Center," *Progressive Architecture*, January, 1984.

"La Casa D'Argento (A Silver House)," *Abitare*, December, 1984, pp. 22–31.

"Lawrence Residence," *GA Houses*, Volume 16, July, 1984.

Webb, Michael. "Verdi Restaurant," *Restaurant and Hotel Design*, May/June, 1984,
pp. 70–73.

Whiteson, Leon. "Gritty 'Venice Vernacular' flows throughout 72 Market Street," *Los Angeles Herald Examiner*, August 28, 1984.

"72 Market Street," *World Stars and Space Design*, 1985.

Brenner, Douglas. "Angeli & 72 Market Street Restaurants," *Architectural Record*, September, 1985, pp. 11, 156–161.

"Los Angeles Becomes the Land of the Unreal," *Buenos Aires Herald*, October, 1985.

"Mayne-Rotondi," *101 Leading Architects*, February, 1985.

"Morphosis," *Axis*, January, 1985.

237

238 "Morphosis," *Modernism Murtuu*, May, 1985.

"Morphosis: Mayne & Rotondi," *International El Croquis*, May, 1985.

"Room to Move," Lawrence Residence and Venice III House," *Progressive Architecture*, August, 1985, pp. 81–92.

"Venice III House," *Progressive Architecture*, January, 1985, pp. 114–115.

Viladas, Pilar. "Work of Morphosis," *GA Houses Special*, May, 1985, pp. 14–83.

"Wanted: View of the Pacific, Lawrence Residence," *Hauser*, April, 1985.

Webb, Michael. "Now for Something Different, Angeli and 72 Market Street Restaurants," *Restaurant and Hotel Design*, March, 1985, pp. 78–82.

"72 Market Street and Angeli Restaurants," *World Stores and Space Design*, Spring, 1986.

"A New Generation of Architects in America," *Emerging Voices*, Fall, 1986, pp. 54–56.

"Around the State-1986 AIA Honor Awards," *California Architecture*, July/August, 1986.

"Building Spareness, Home Design," *New York Times*, September 21, 1986.

"California AIA Awards," *Architecture California*, April, 1986, p. 13.

"Designers in the Front Line of Architecture," *Los Angeles Herald Examiner, California Living*, August 31, 1986.

Goldberger, Paul. "Venice III," *California*, September, 1986.

McNair, Andrew. "Forty Under Forty," *Interiors*, September, 1986.

"Morphosis Projects as Photographed by Tim Street Porter," *L.A. Houses*, Fall, 1986.

"The New High Style Hospital, C.C.C.," *Newsweek*, July 28, 1986.

"On Being Hip in Venice with Conviction," *Architecture*, May, 1986.

Drohojowska, Hunter. "An Appetite for Design," *L.A. Style*, August, 1986, p. 73.

Searle, Judith. "Archistyle," *Main Magazine*, January/February, 1986.

"Un Castello Immaginario, Venice III," *Abitare*, September, 1986.

"Update: Top Designers," *Restaurant & Hotel Design*, June, 1986, p. 92.

"Venice III," *A.M.C., Revue D'Architecture*, October, 1986, pp. 38–39.

"1987 Design Awards," *L.A. Architect*, December, 1987, pp. 1–3.

"Ambiente in Los Angeles," *Ambiente*, May, 1987, p. 12.

"Architect Shops," *The Los Angeles Business Journal*, November 2, 1987.

Betsky, Aaron. "The Emerging Generation in U.S.A.," *GA Houses Special*, November, 1987, pp. 14–21.

"Big Fish, Little Quirks," Clinch Design Awards for L.A.'s Small Avant-Garde

"The Crowd at Kate's," *Traveler*, November, 1987, pp. 26–27.

Fitoussi, Brigitte. "Steak House a Beverly Hills," *L'Architecture D'Aujourd'Hui*, December, 1987, pp. 84–86.

Giovannini, Joseph. "For a New Los Angeles Style, A Place in the Sun," *New York Times*, April 16, 1987, pp. C1, C6.

"Mega Morphosis," *L.A. Style*, July, 1987, pp. 50–56.

"Klapper, Zina. "But Will it Prescribe Espresso I.V.'s?," *California Business*, November, 1987.

"Los Angeles Architecture," *Los Angeles Times*, March 14, 1987.

"Malibu Beach House, 6th Street, Crawford House," *Daidalos*, December, 1987, pp. 72–75.

Moore, Rowan. "Duchamp Goes West," *Blueprint*, Number 37, May, 1987, pp. 18–20.

"New Light on L.A.," *The Architectural Review*, December, 1987, pp. 14–21.

"Morphosis: Play Sculpter/Conceptual Orrery," *AA Files*, Number 14, Spring, 1987, pp. 14–17.

Rand, George. "Design and the Experience of Dining, 72 Market Street," *Architecture*, April, 1987, pp. 72–74.

Rethlake, Kathy. "Winning Design," *The Evening Outlook*, November 30, 1987, p. B1.

"Sixth Street Residence," *Oz*, Volume 9, 1987, pp. 12–15.

"Venice III" *Abitare*, October, 1987.

"6th Street," *ADPSR*, 1988, p. 13.

"35th Annual P/A Awards," January, 1988, pp. 116–117.

Abercrombie, Stanley. "Vecta Tempo Showroom, PDC," *Interior Design*, August, 1988, pp. 166–167.

Bates, Betsy. "L.A.'s After-Hours Cancer Clinic," *Los Angeles Herald Examiner*, January 14, 1988, p. 43.

Bissell, Terry. "Lifeguard Tower," *Main Magazine*, Volume 3, No. 1, Sept./Oct./Nov./1988.

Boles, Daralice D. "Architecture's Rising Star," *Elle*, April, 1988, p. 286.

"CCAIA Merit Award" *Architectural California*, Volume 10, No.3, May/June, 1988, p. 24.

"Connotation and Denotation, Morphosis: Three Projects," *The University of Tennessee Journal of Architecture*, Volume 10, 1988, pp. 22–23.

"Deconstruction in Architecture," *Architectural Design*, Volume 58, No. 3/4, 1988, pp. 76–80.

"A Food Hall at the Entrance to Beverly Hills," *Abitare*, Number 261, January/February, 1988, pp. 174–183.

Gakin, Julie. "Dream House: A Place of One's Own," *Diversion*, April, 1988, p. 275.

Gardener, Elizabeth. "Comprehensive Cancer Center," *Modern Health Care*, October, 1988, p. 40.

Inspiration, Inspiration, 1988, pp. 56–57.

Israel, Frank. "Representation," *Via*, (Journal of the Graduate School of Fine Arts, University of Pennsylvania), Volume 9, 1988, pp. 27–38.

Kaiser, Christoph. "Berlin–Denkmal oder Denkmodell?," *Journal*, September, 1988, p. 17.

Kaplan, Sam Hall. "Award Rhetoric, Building Realities," Part VIII, *Los Angeles Times*, May 22, 1988, p. 82.

"Kate Mantilini, 2468 House, Prototype Hamburger Stand," Design World, No. 15, 1988, pp. 42–43.

Knox, Barbara J. "Goldins Rule," *Lighting Dimensions*, April, 1988, pp. 46–49, 65–69.

"Lifeguard Tower," *Progressive Architecture*, August, 1988.

Lifton, Sarah. "Architects of Ideas: Michael Rotondi Puts Design on a Higher Plane," *Angeles*, December, 1988, pp. 76–79.

"Malibu House," *Sunset*, October, 1988, p. 62.

"P/A in July," *Progressive Architecture*, June, 1988.

Pastier, John. "Stylish Space For a Celebrity Restaurant," May, 1988, pp. 129–181.

Schlinke, Britton. "The Pleasures of Complexity," *Artweek*, Volume 19, No. 34, October 15, 1988, p. 15.

"'Sibernes' Haus in Los Angeles," *MD (Moebel Interior Design)*, Volume 10, October, 1988, pp. 100–110.

Stein, John. "Scene Stealer," *Architectural Record*, May, 1988, pp. 132–135.

Suisman, Doug. "Contradictions of Care," *Architectural Review*, June, 1988, pp. 26–31.

Temko, Suzanah. "Westside Builds a Reputation," Life/Arts, *The Evening Outlook*, April 28, 1988, pp. D1, 2G.

Tonsager, Ved Svein. "Morphosis: A Conversation with Michael Rotondi of the Californian Architecure Office," *Skala*, September, 1988, pp. 12–17.

"Twelve by Twelve," *L.A. Architect*, March, 1988.

Viladas, Pilar. "The Road to Recovery," *Progressive Architecture*, July, 1988, pp. 67–75.

"West Coast Wise Guys," *Home*, September, 1988, pp. 60–66.

White, Garrett. "Sci-Arc," *L.A. Style*, September, 1988.

Bachman, Wolfgang; Mathewson, M.; Casey, C. "Los Angeles, Paradise and Limbo," "A House is a House is a House," *Bauwelt*, April, 1989, pp. 736, 744–745, 767–769, 774–777.

Bartsch-Rudiger, Marina; Muller, Alois Martin. "Vers une architecture de la difference, and Berlin-Denkmal oder Denkmodell?," *Archithese*, January, 1989, pp. 10–19.

"Berlin Wall," *Redbook*, 14X A-9, "Library Competition."

Betsky, Aaron. "Architecture: Steel Chic and Stucco Dreams at the L.A. Lab," *Metropolitan Home*, August 1989, pp. 75–87.

Campbell, Robert. "Recapturing the Creative World of Play," *The Boston Sunday Globe*, July 16, 1989, p. B-1.

Cohn, David. "Recent Work," *El Croquis*, January, 1989, pp. 10–19.

"Comprehensive Cancer Center," *GA Document*, Volume 22, January 22, 1989, pp. 56–69.

"Comprehensive Cancer Clinic," *GA Document*, Volume 12, January, 1989, pp. 128–133.

Contemporary Architecture 10, 1988–1989, pp. 116–121.

"Crawford House," *Progressive Architecture*, January, 1989, pp. 84–85.

"Off Beat L.A." and "Der Dekonstruktivismus," *Archithese*, February, 1989, pp. 41–48, 62.

Phillips, Patricia. *Morphosis: A Decade of Architectural Confrontation, 1989.*

Rand, George. "Morphosis: Three Houses (Walker Arts Center)," *Architecture Tomorrow*, May, 1989.

Wagner, George. *Thom Mayne-Sixth Street House*, 1989.

239

1988
Stephanie Adolph
Kiyokazu Arai
Debbie Berg
Cathleen Chua
Robin Donaldson
John Enright
Karen Frome
Jill Goldberg
Mauricio Gomez
Kim Groves
Barbara Helton-Berg
Caroline Hench
Steve Johnson
Shiou-Hee Ko
Mehran Mashayekh
Jason Macdonald-Hall
Thom Mayne
Mark McVay
Bethe Munns
Kanika R'Kul
Michael Rotondi
Will Sharp
Maya Shimoguchi
Clark Stevens
Steve Suchman
Remko Van Buren
Dukho Yeon
Gideon Zadoks
Ann Zollinger

240

1987
Kiyokazu Arai
Craig Burdick
Rich Brinser
Robert Churchill
Andrea Claire
Robin Donaldson
John Enright
Jill Goldberg
Mauricio Gomez
David Guthrie
Barbara Helton-Berg
Caroline Hench
Selwyn Ting
Bill Huang
Steve Johnson
Susan Lanier
Tom Lasley
Tom Marble
Mehran Mashayekh
Thom Mayne
Martin Roy Mervel
Bethe Munns
Katie Philips
Kanika R'Kul
Michael Rotondi
Michael Sant
Will Sharp

1987
Maya Shimoguchi
Clark Stevens
Steve Suchman
Vivian Wang
Remko Van Buren
Gideon Zadoks
Ann Zollinger

1986
Kiyokazu Arai
Barbara Bester
Brian Blaschke
Craig Burdick
David Davis
Robin Donaldson
John Dutton
Mauricio Gomez
Kim Groves
Barbara Helton-Berg
Annette Hoehn
Mara Hochman
Patrick Hurpin
Steve Johnson
Bob Josten
Eric Kahn
Thom Mayne
Martin Mervel
Bethe Munns
Lou Perron
Truit Roberts
Michael Rotondi
Mahmood Michele Saie
Charlie Scott
Joey Shimoda
Maya Shimoguchi
Tim Swischuk
Christopher Tandon
Chris Uebel
Andrew Zago

1985
Kiyokazu Arai
Florence Bleecher
Robin Donaldson
Kim Groves
Eric Kahn
Brendon Macfarlane
Thom Mayne
Kathy Rea
Michael Rotondi
Alex Rudeneau
Mahmood Michele Saie
Raquel Vert

1984
Kiyokazu Arai
Tony Bell
Florence Bleecher
Robin Donaldson
Carol Hove
Eric Kahn
Brendan Macfarlane
Thom Mayne
Michael Rotondi
Alexandra Rudeneau

1983
Tom Adolf
Kiyokazu Arai
Tony Bell
Florence Bleecher
Brad Caplow
Ron Fiala
Bill Huang
Randy Jacobson
Joseph Ma
Neal Matsano
Martin Roy Mervel
Thom Mayne
Michael Rotondi
Mahmood Michele Saie
Jay Vanos
Raquel Vert

1982
Kiyokazu Arai
Hannah Banks
Tony Bell
Isabel Brones
Ben Caffey
Bradley Caplow
Barbara Helton-Berg
Bill Huang
Gianluigi Irsonti
Randy Jacobson
Joseph Ma
Thom Mayne
Judith Newmark
Margaretha Nilsson
Michael Rotondi
Alexandra Rudeneau
Mahmood Michele Saie
Tom Scarin
Barry Segal
Sam Shabazi
Raquel Vert

1981
Kiyokazu Arai
Thom Mayne
Ben Caffey
Joseph Ma
Judith Newmark
Michael Rotondi
Jeff Warn

1980
Kiyokazu Arai
Hannah Banks
Jo Duda
Ron Fiala
Ankie Krisbolder
Ben Caffey
Frank Lupo
Joseph Ma
Thom Mayne
Judith Newmark
Michael Rotondi
Marlou Veugelers
Gene Watanabe

1979
Ron Fiala
Linda Lee
Frank Lupo
Joseph Ma
Thom Mayne
Judith Newmark
Michael Rotondi

1978
Linda Lee
Thom Mayne
Michael Rotondi

1977
Rick Clemenson
Gary Farber
Linda Lee.
Laurie Levenson
Frank Lupo
Thom Mayne
Richard Orne
Ruben Ojeda
Michael Rotondi
Livio Santini
John Souza

1976
Pete Bocato
Lise Mathews
Thom Mayne
Michael Rotondi
Gary Russel
Livio Santini
James Takamune

1975
Thom Mayne
Michael Rotondi
Luis Perez
Livio Santini
James Takamune
Martin Wagner

1974
Thom Mayne
Michael Rotondi

1973
Michael Brickler
Thom Mayne
Michael Rotondi
James Stafford